ALLEN H. WOOD, JR.

TRY THESE INDOORS

A HANDBOOK OF
UNUSUAL HOUSE PLANTS
ILLUSTRATED

BOSTON ∾ 1941

HALE, CUSHMAN & FLINT

PERUVIAN LILY (*Alstroemeria chilensis*). Page 34

CONTENTS

LIST OF PHOTOGRAPHS

INTRODUCTION

I NDOOR gardening is not a new practice. Geraniums and begonias and fuchsias were cherished in the homes of our great-grandmothers, and their forbears, too. Yet something in the past decade has given tremendous impetus to the hobby of window gardening. Not only have indoor plantings increased in number, the *type* of garden has changed also. Where, not so long ago, there was marked standardization of plant material grown in the average collection, it is not a fact today. Indoor gardeners have become individualists instead of mimics: they have acquired an experimental strain.

In a previous house plant book, "Grow Them Indoors," I included descriptions of a number of plants which proved to be strangers to many indoor gardeners. Numerous letters were sent to me asking for more information about these plants; and for lists of other unusual subjects which may be grown in a window garden or conservatory.

This book is in answer to the many letters of inquiry and, I hope, the unspoken curiosity of other window gardeners who find interest and satisfaction in growing plants unknown to them at present. "Try These Indoors" is a handbook of unusual and seldom-grown house plants.

Not all the plants described in the book are as complacent in behavior as are some of the old favorites; yet all may be cultivated successfully in most window gardens. Where special care or conditions are necessary they are explained in full. And, with very few exceptions, all plants listed are available in this country.

I am grateful to Messrs. Ross Chase, J. N. Giridlian, Carl C. Fraser, Frank White, Walter Beebe Wilder, James Esson, and Frank Oeschlin for their respective co-operation in the matter of photographs: and to Messrs. Rex D. Pearce and John Gallagher for numerous line drawings. Mr. E. I. Farrington of the Massachusetts Horticultural Society courteously extended the privilege to quote from the Society's magazine "Horticulture," which I have done in several instances. Also I wish to thank Houghton Mifflin and Macmillan for permission to use excerpts from "The Garden Dictionary" and "Garden Cinderellas."

ALLEN H. WOOD, JR.

Boston, 1940

I

POTTING — LIGHTING — WATERING

Chapter 1

POTTING—LIGHTING—WATERING

House plants require containers which, for the most part, will be ordinary clay flower pots. These are available in sizes graduating from miniature 'thimble' pots to large individuals 14 inches across. Certain house plants that require even larger containers may be planted in wooden tubs or bowls of glazed pottery which come in a wide range of sizes and shapes.

Either old or new clay pots may be utilized. Old ones should be scrubbed thoroughly before being used again, in order to dispose of caked potting soil and ancient fungous growths. When new pots are contemplated, they should be soaked in water for at least 24 hours to saturate the clay completely. Otherwise it will absorb moisture which is intended for the plant's feeding roots, and make it difficult to establish the newly potted specimen.

Glazed pots are enjoying increasing popularity. In comparing the older type of clay pot with more recent kinds, much has been said pro and con. As a matter of fact, both are suitable for use with house plants. Many of the glazed pots come without drainage holes. In this instance additional drainage material must be placed beneath the potting soil (see Fig. 1). Leaving aside any scientific discussion of comparative merits, the greatest asset of glazed containers is aesthetic. Clay pots are clay pots, obtainable in one color only —brick red. The other type has definite style. Infinite colors and shapes are available, that by intelligent handling may be made to become component parts of planned planting pictures.

Condition and species of specimen will determine when to plant. The best time is just after growth has commenced. At this time roots are in prime condition to withstand the shock of transplanting. When a plant is resting, the roots, too, are dormant. Potting at this time often finds the plant's vitality too low to become established in new surroundings.

In potting plants, a common fault is the use of a larger container than is necessary. This results in overwatering, sour soil, and sparse or complete absence of flowers. Under-potting is preferable always to overpotting. In plants of the amaryllis family, and with some members of the lily family, roots must be potbound before the plant will produce flowers. Nothing is to be gained by providing roots with more soil than they can use advantageously.

Like all planting operations, soil should be packed firmly around the roots of newly potted plants. There is a happy medium, however, for soil rammed into a pot until it is almost as solid as the container itself is incorrect procedure. Such a condition prevents circulation of water and air, both of which are essential to healthy normal growth.

Particular attention should be accorded provision for

drainage. While water is the agent through which food in the soil is made available to plant roots, improper use of it packs and sours soil, excludes all air, and soon causes rot to appear in roots and bulbs.

Drainage holes are incorporated in bottoms of clay pots and many glazed containers. These vents, however, are by no means all that is necessary to provide adequate drainage. If nothing but soil is placed in the containers, water soon washes it into the hole where it forms a plug that seals the pot and causes a complete cessation of drainage. Other means are necessary. Therefore, over the bottom of the pot, place a layer of pebbles, gravel, or broken pieces of other flower pots. An inch or so of sphagnum moss placed over the drainage layer before the potting soil is added will prevent the soil from washing down through the pebbles. Naturally the size of the pot will determine the depth of the drainage layer. If you will make it twice the depth you at first consider, it will be about right.

As mentioned previously, containers which are not provided with vents need more drainage material than those which have bottom holes. A good procedure to follow in this instance is to use one-third drainage area and two-thirds potting soil. Even with this precaution water never must be allowed to accumulate above the drainage stratum, or a soggy mess will result.

Most house plant containers are placed in saucers or bowls to protect table tops and window sills from water trickling through bottom vents. Fill these supplementary vessels partly with pebbles. Then no harm can come to the plant

if overflow remains, for the pot is supported on pebbles above
the water. A few pieces of charcoal mixed with the pebbles
will keep surplus drainage clean and odorless.

Perhaps all the emphasis upon drainage may sound re-
dundant, yet it is an extremely important factor in successful house plant culture. House plant ills are blamed upon
many things; actually most of them are directly traceable to
improper drainage.

When plants are potted in the spring most of them will
be benefited by plunging them in the garden, or a suitable
outdoor spot, during the warm summer months. Be sure
to leave them in the containers; otherwise the root systems
are apt to increase to a size which will make it difficult to
repot in the fall without severely pruning the root structure.

Ventilation is another factor which affects indoor culture.
Plants which have been potted recently, repotted, or have
summered in the garden should be acclimated to house atmosphere gradually, not abruptly. This may be accomplished by returning plants to the house well in advance
of the onset of cold weather. Leave as many windows open
for two or three weeks as is practical; this enables plants to
adjust themselves slowly to house conditions.

Fresh air is required summer and winter. Even during
midwinter months, windows should be opened daily for
five or ten minutes. Not where a blast of frigid air will blow
directly upon the window garden, of course, yet near enough
so the plants will get the benefit of fresh, vitalized air. Care
and discretion must be exercised, for many plants are very

tender and even a breath of frost will injure them irreparably.

A satisfactory temperature for the growth of many plants in the average house does not present a major problem. While it is a fact that certain species require slow growth in a cool location, and others demand warmth and high humidity, the larger number find a temperature between 60 and 68 degrees quite satisfactory. Where special growing conditions are required, it is possible usually to find some place in the house which meets the need.

Plants growing in native habitats usually find after-dark temperatures lower than during the day. In the house they do better when the temperature is lowered about 10 degrees at night.

Regarding light, watering, and food, I repeat from "Grow Them Indoors" for the benefit of those who have not read the detailed growing instructions contained therein.

Light may be considered in two ways, with sunshine and without. Certain plants, like ivies and ferns, grow without benefit of direct rays of the sun; yet flowering plants insist upon sun if they are going to bloom. Light is a primary necessity for house plants. Without it growth is puny and weak or lacking entirely. Specimens which are etiolated or enervated through lack of it become easy prey for insects and fungous diseases. Light is a priceless ingredient in the complex chemical process which results in healthy foliage and brilliant flowers.

The necessary amount of light varies with different plants, as you would expect. Most house plants, and all flowering

VARIOUS POTTING PROCEDURES

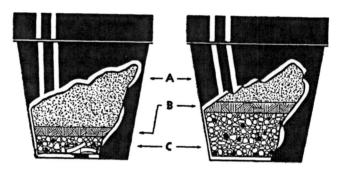

CONTENTS OF POTS WITH AND WITHOUT VENTS

A. POTTING SOIL

B. SPHAGNUM MOSS

C. DRAINAGE LAYER

Note that drainage layer in unvented pot is much deeper

PEBBLES KEEP POT ABOVE
SURPLUS DRAINAGE WATER

DOUBLE POTTING WITH MOSS
OR PEAT MOSS IN OUTER CON-
TAINER KEEPS INNER POT MOIST

FIG. I

kinds, as well as cacti and succulents, do best in windows or exposures facing the south. Eastern windows are indifferently satisfactory and western exposures, poor.

While sun is so very important to budding plants, often it bleaches and shortens the life of flowers after they have opened. It helps bright flowers to move the plants just out of direct sunlight during the blossoming period.

Light and water are the two main sources of plant nourishment: light for the process of photosynthesis by which leaves manufacture starch and sugar, and water through whose agency mineral salts and soil foods are made available to roots. Both light and water are necessary, because they are component parts of the plant's starch and sugar factory.

It is impractical, if not impossible, to make any specific statement as to the amount of water plants require, as the factors which enter into the matter are too numerous and variable. For instance, a plant growing in a moist atmosphere at a temperature of 60 degrees requires far less water than the same plant situated in a hot, dry atmosphere. Escape of water through leaf pores varies widely according to heat and humidity. Naturally the faster water is evaporated through leaves the sooner roots require an additional supply.

We do know that plants require less water during the dormant or resting phase than they do when in active growth. We are cognizant also of the fact that certain species demand more moisture than others. Plants in clay pots dry out more rapidly than do the same plants in non-porous glazed containers; and sunny days cause more evaporation than do dull ones. So you see there are many things to be considered.

By and large, a fairly safe guide for watering plants in the house is to watch the pot and its soil contents. When a clay pot is very light in color, and the soil is powdery and dry to the touch, a need of water is apparent. You will have to determine a watering schedule for such plants as you grow in accordance with species and conditions of light, temperature, and humidity in *your* house. Daily inspection is helpful, and you will soon find that the fulfilling of each plant's needs is much easier than it sounds.

Humidity is a great help in the culture of house plants; most of them are grateful for a moist atmosphere. If you live in a home which is properly air conditioned, the problem is no problem. Otherwise some provision should be made to evaporate water in the vicinity of the plants.

Grow lots of paper-white narcissi, golden-yellow narcissi, and hyacinths in pebbles and water near your other plants; they are lovely in the house and the water they are rooted in adds to the moisture content of surrounding air. Radiator pans full of water are useful, and large vessels of water may be tucked in out-of-the-way corners—all add to the humidity. Where practical, zinc pans, 3 inches deep, built to fit window sills, shelves, and bay window areas, may be filled to the top with pebbles and an inch of water kept in the bottom. Flower pots rest on the surface of the pebbles well above the water; yet moisture is there, actively contributing its bit to better growing conditions. And don't forget to spray plants with tepid water regularly and often (exceptions will be noted under separate listings).

When watering is indicated, supply the need thoroughly. Moisture which penetrates only an inch or so is worse than no water at all. It is the roots near the bottom of the pot which are clamoring for water, not the stem of the plant at the surface. Don't give plants the shivers or a bad chill by dousing them with very cold water, such as comes from a faucet in the middle of winter. Keep the water—or make it —as near room temperature as possible, and apply until water runs out of the bottom vent. In large specimens it is difficult sometimes to be sure that the entire contents of the pot is soaked completely. Such plants are best plunged into a pail of water once a week, and allowed to remain there until moist top soil indicates that the plant has absorbed its fill. Have the height of water in the pail about one-half that of the pot which is to be plunged into it.

A method of catering to particularly thirsty plants is shown in Figure 1E. The pot containing the plant is set in a larger container and the space between filled with sphagnum moss or peat moss. When the material is kept wet constantly, the potting mixture in the smaller pot is assured of continual moisture without danger of flooding. If the inner pot is filled with sand instead of soil it becomes a small, yet efficient, rooting place for cuttings.

Leaf pores should be open, for through them the plant breathes as well as transpires water. Even the most meticulous housekeeper cannot prevent the intrusion of dust. It will settle on foliage and seal the pores unless removed from time to time. Removal is best accomplished by spraying leaves with water. Once a week the entire plant may be placed under a faucet and given a good bath while lying on its side in the sink. Also, the procedure is an excellent anti-dote for red spider, mealybug, and aphis. Leaf washing should not be employed with downy-leaved plants and ferns.

Until clinging drops of water have disappeared, plants recently washed or sprayed should be protected from direct sun rays by drawn shades or other means. Each drop of water is a small magnifying glass. Sun rays brought to a focus through surface beads of water often severely scorch and burn leaves and flowers.

Plant life requires nourishment. Certain plants, like people, have larger appetites than others. Aside from quantities involved, all plants extract whatever plant food, good or bad, is to be found in the soil wherein the roots are buried. Constant draining, without refilling, will empty anything. When the food value of potting soil is gone it requires replenishing. When and how to do this, then, is the question.

Plants purchased at greenhouses or florists will not need additional feeding for several months at least; probably longer, as the soil in which they are planted has been fertilized amply. The potting mixtures referred to in this book also will take care of the food question for a number of months.

When there is something noticeably wrong with a plant; when it ceases to grow, foliage yellows, or leaves droop and drop, it *may* be from lack of plant food. On the other hand, the chances are ten to one that the ailment can be traced to some other cause. Overwatering, for instance, improperly functioning drainage, potbound roots, or insect pests. If all these things have been checked and given a clean bill of health—then fertilize. It is a not uncommon tendency to blame every plant ill on lack of food, with the result that plants are overfed grossly and die. Better, by far, to supply too little than too much. When plants are in a dormant or resting phase, leaves not quite so green, and no new shoots appear, enthusiastic gardeners are apt to feel that a little additional feeding might be welcome. The intent is kindly; yet plants truly need the rest, and fertilizing at this time is harmful, not beneficial.

Flowering plants require more fertilizer than foliage plants as a rule. Occasional applications of manure water during the budding period are helpful. With most plants two or three feedings a year are sufficient. When a plant is fed, water it before and after the operation; this negates any tendency to burn the roots. Bone meal makes an excellent top dressing as it does not burn and its assimilation is slower than most commercial fertilizers, many of which are quick-acting. It is the safest plant food to use with bulbs in particular; but not with azaleas or other plants of the heath family which dislike the lime contained in bone meal.

Potting mixtures include dried cow manure, bone meal, or both. Under no circumstances use fresh animal manures of any kind; they invariably scorch the plant. Plant tablets, advertised and sold by reputable companies, are practical and convenient. Also there are a number of balanced foods and mineral salts on the market which are obtainable in bags and cartons; they are efficient and safe if the application is guided by accompanying printed instructions.

In the matter of feeding, as in watering, common sense and familiarity with different plant subjects are twin assets which connote success.

House plants necessitate supervision and trimming to

keep them shapely, to prevent them from becoming lop-sided or leggy or tangled. Bulbous plants, however, seldom require this attention; for they grow, flower, and then enter a rest period at which time the foliage in most species dies off.

Plants have a marked affinity for the sun; they will reach toward it inevitably. Unless something is done to counteract this congenital yearning, all plants in the window or near the window will assume a most unattractive angle. It is easy enough to prevent the asymmetrical results of this solar worship by giving the pots a quarter turn every two or three days. Growth then becomes even on all sides.

II

AMARYLLIS FAMILY

Chapter 2

AMARYLLIS FAMILY

P LANTS of the amaryllis family are of major importance to indoor gardeners. Comprised mostly of tropical bulbous herbs, the family offers a splendid array of subjects for window gardens. Although such species as snowdrop, snowflake, narcissus, and lycoris are entirely hardy in outdoor plantings, it is the more tender amaryllids which are of interest here.

One member only of the group bears the name amaryllis; it is the belladonna lily from South Africa, *Amaryllis belladonna;* although the name is used frequently in conjunction with South American hippeastrums.

Certain characteristics are quite general throughout this large plant family. Cognizance should be taken of them to assure satisfactory cultivation. For instance, root structures are injured easily. Therefore transplant or repot just as seldom as possible. Planting in large containers results in abundant leaf growth, and few or no flowers. Use small pots with all amaryllids; that is, small for the size of the plant, for cramped roots are essential to production of buds and the

31

lily-like flowers for which amaryllids are noted. Here applications of horticultural Vitamin B1 are of assistance.

Various species and varieties agree in requiring a rest of several months after flowering, although some of the plants are evergreen. Before the rest period, leaves of non-evergreen species must be grown on and developed in order to ripen bulbs properly.

2 parts loam
2 parts leaf mold
2 parts sand
½ part old cow manure
Sprinkling of bone meal

AMARYLLIS POTTING MIXTURE

Unlike hardy bulbous plants, such as tulip, hyacinth, lily, and narcissus, which must be placed in a dark cold place for a month or more to root, amaryllids have a fondness for warmth and light. They will start root growth immediately after potting when given proper growing conditions.

Not the least of attributes found in this group is the fact that plants may be kept in the same containers year after year, gaining in size and beauty with the passing of time.

Very infrequent repotting is required, as necessary resting periods may be provided by laying the pots on their sides in a warm dry cellar or similar location. Fresh dirt dug into the pot yearly, and occasional applications of manure water will keep the plants contented and well fed.

Many amaryllids are distinguished by bulbs with long stout necks. These, and the upper curve of the expanded part of the bulb always should be left extending above the potting soil. And another thing! Bulbs in this division usually produce offsets, other bulbs and bulblets in varying sizes. Leave them attached to the mother bulb until they separate of their own accord. They resent a hurried or forced parting from parental protection.

While specific descriptions and cultural instructions will be found under each genus, the following formula for potting soil may be adhered to except where noted: two parts garden loam; two parts leaf mold; two parts potting sand (use sharp sand, not beach sand); one-half part old and dried cow manure; a liberal sprinkling of bone meal. Be sure the potting mixture components are mixed thoroughly.

Manure water has been mentioned as an added stimulant. This may be obtained by soaking a cloth bag of cow or sheep manure in a bucket of water. Do not use hen manure, as it is too powerful and caustic unless very old and partially leached.

ALSTROEMERIA

Peruvian lilies comprise about 50 species of South American plants, amaryllis family, of which a number are in cultivation as subjects for growing in the garden, greenhouse, and as house plants. They grow from fibrous or tuberous roots attached to a crown from which arise leafy stalks bearing the flower clusters. Leaves are narrow and often twisted at the base. Mostly spring-flowering.

DESCRIPTION: *Alstroemeria aurantiaca.* The numerous, lance-shaped leaves are about 4 inches long, growing in a whorl under the flower cluster, scattered elsewhere. The flowers are yellow, tipped with green, and spotted with brown.

ALSTROEMERIA

Alstroemeria chilensis. Leaves are bluish-green and fringed; not as numerous as in *A. aurantiaca.* The flowers are carried on 3 foot stalks. In color they are rose-red or whitish and are fewer in number than in above species.

Alstroemeria pelegrina. Called Lily of the Incas. Flowers are dark rose, inner petals spotted with rose-purple. The large umbel is carried on 12-18 inch stalks. A variety, *alba,* has spotted, sometimes unspotted, white flowers of great beauty.

CULTURE: The roots of alstroemeria are very easily damaged and require care in handling when shipped and planted.

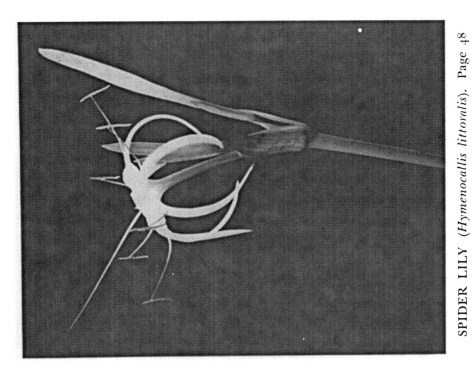

SPIDER LILY (*Hymenocallis littoralis*). Page 48

Cyrtanthus lutescens. Page 44

FLAMINGO FLOWER (*Anthurium scherzerianum*).
Page 61

BLACK CALLA (*Arum palaestinum*). Page 62

The potting mixture should consist of equal parts of rich loam, sharp sand, and humus. Provide ample drainage material. Pot in the fall, give very little water until growth commences, then water regularly. After the flowering period, gradually reduce watering as the plant ripens, and give but small amounts until growth starts again the next fall. Do not disturb plantings until absolutely necessary.

AMARCRINUM

Many window gardens have been brightened by the rosy flowers of *Amaryllis belladonna;* a few have known the blossoms of crinum. Now *A. belladonna* and *Crinum moorei* have been wedded by a grower named Howard, and a true bi-generic hybrid is available. It is called *Amarcrinum howardi.*

DESCRIPTION: Grows from a large bulb. The leaves are strap-shaped and evergreen. Large, fragrant, funnel-shaped flowers of soft, satiny pink are borne on sturdy, 3 foot stalks. The plants naturally bloom during the summer, yet in the house they will flower earlier or later depending upon when they are planted.

CULTURE: Use the general potting mixture as described for amaryllids. If only one bulb is used to a pot, choose a container of a size which will allow 2 inches of soil between the outside of the bulb and rim of pot. If more than one bulb is planted to a pot, use the single planting as a basis for container size.

After planting, place the pot in a rather cool, semi-dark room until top-growth becomes active. Then bring into the light for growing on. Use manure water every two or three weeks during the growing season. After the plants have attained maximum size, flowered, and flourished for a month thereafter, lay the pot on its side in a warm cellar for ninety days in order to rest the plant. Do not withhold water entirely, but supply only enough to keep the bulb plump and the foliage from drying off completely.

AMMOCHARIS

This splendid plant is practically a stranger to window gardens in this country. As a pot or tub plant it offers a striking and lovely subject. While several species are available, *Ammocharis falcata* is probably the best; although *Ammocharis coccinea* is grown extensively in European window gardens.

DESCRIPTION: Grows from a bulb. The leaves are 1-2 feet in length, strap-shaped, and often lie quite flat. Flowers are red and very fragrant, lily-like in shape, many in a ball-shaped cluster on a short, stout stalk. Outdoors, ammocharis blooms in the summer; earlier when grown inside. Flowering is variable depending upon the planting schedule.

CULTURE: The same as for amarcrinum, but use one-third more sand in the potting mixture.

ANIGOZANTHUS

Amaryllids from Australia of definite interest as pot plants. While the flowers are quite lovely, the bright green, iris-like leaves have a year around appeal. Flowers and flower stalks are covered with a yellow or red woolly pubescence which is both interesting and decorative.

DESCRIPTION: *Anigozanthus flavida.* Also called kangaroo paws. The plant grows from a fleshy rootstock, not a bulb. Leaves are basal mostly, narrow, and evergreen. The tubular yellow flowers are borne in much-branched racemes on 3-4 foot stalks. Yellow pubescence. The normal flowering period is May to June.

Anigozanthus manglesi. This species is similar to *A. flavida,* but the woolly flowers are red with green at the base of the petals.

CULTURE: General amaryllis culture and potting mixture. Supply ample water in spring and diminish supply during the winter. Additional plants may be obtained by root divisions made in the spring.

BRAVOA

A small and little-known amaryllid genus from the tablelands of Central Mexico, where the plants grow at an altitude of from 5000-8000 feet. Most species resemble the tuberose (*Polianthes tuberosa*). Slender stems arise from small thickened rootstocks. The grayish-green leaves, which are ½-¾ inch wide, and 12-18 inches long, are mostly basal. Flowers occur in pairs on 18-24 inch spikes or racemes, which has given the genus its common name, Mexican twin-flower. Blossoms appear in early summer. Growth starts in late winter and matures in the fall. While about 8 species have been described, one only is in cultivation.

DESCRIPTION: *Bravoa geminiflora.* Grows from a rootstock. The bright, coral-red, tubular flowers, 20-30 in number, hang in pairs on the flower stalk.

CULTURE: Plant the rootstock in early winter in regular amaryllis potting mixture. Give it two weeks in a dark cool location. Then treat in the same manner as cyrtanthus.

BUPHANE

Plants in this genus are interesting and unique rather than beautiful. The flowers are crowded in ball-shaped umbels atop short heavy stalks, and the general effect is one of large red or purple balloons.

DESCRIPTION: *Buphane disticha.* Grows from a very large bulb. The leaves are leathery, either lance- or tongue-shaped, from 1-1½ feet in length, with hairy margins. The flowers are exceedingly numerous and, in this species, rose-red.

CULTURE: Provide lots of drainage and add one part of peat to the general amaryllis potting mixture. Water sparingly until top-growth starts. When the foliage begins to dry off, cease watering entirely. Before resting the plant, give the bulb a long thorough drying in the sun, with provision to keep it from being rained upon. Weak manure water benefits during the growing season.

CLIVIA

The older species and varieties of this most dependable plant are no strangers to window gardens and conservatories.

The large clusters of flowers in shades of apricot and orange are perennial favorites. Once clivia is established it persists for years even with indifferent treatment. Large specimens may be grown in tubs. Most often seen and grown is the species, *Clivia miniata*. In addition to this popular and colorful stand-by, there are several other lesser known species and some beautiful hybrids which deserve to be known better.

DESCRIPTION: Grows from an imperfect bulb consisting of expanded leaf bases. The numerous leaves are evergreen, thick, and variously strap-shaped. The shape of the flowers is lily-like. They grow in clusters, each flower measuring 2-3 inch in length. The umbels are carried on stout stalks, and flowers remain in bloom for a long time. Flowering is in early spring.

Clivia nobilis. The flowers are reddish-yellow, tipped with green. There are as many as 30 flowers in each umbel.

Clivia cyrtanthiflora. A lovely hybrid, with huge clusters of orange and green flowers.

Clivia miniata, hybrids. The flowers open wider and flatter than in the case of the species, and are shaded lighter in coloring.

Clivia nobilis, hybrids. The leaves are wider and blunter than in *miniata* hybrids. Flowers range from light to dark orange-red in color.

Clivia, Zimmerman hybrids. A group of splendid hybrid clivias showing *miniata* traits in the narrow pointed leaves and pastel flower colors.

CULTURE: The same as for amarcrinum, but work a little peat moss into the potting mixture.

COOPERIA

The rain or prairie lily, as it is called, is a native of south-western United States and Mexico. This night-blooming bulbous herb responds magically to water during the growing season; for in its habitat it produces a succession of flowers after each fall of rain. While here described as a plant for indoor gardens, cooperia may be grown out of doors as far north as Massachusetts if the bulbs are lifted and stored each fall. Although the flowers are fully expanded only after dark, they remain partly open during the day.

SPREKELIA   COOPERIA

DESCRIPTION: Grows from a bulb. The leaves are grass-like, basal, and twisted usually. Flowers are funnel-shaped, fragrant, and solitary at end of stalk. Beneath each flower is a tubular or funnel-shaped bract. The plant is summer-blooming, although alternate watering and drying off will produce successive crops of flowers.

Cooperia drummondi. On hollow, rather frail stalks about 1 foot in height, single flowers, 3-5 inches in length, are carried in solitary glory. The blossoms are white, tinged with red, and scented deliciously. The narrow leaves seldom exceed 12 inches in length.

Cooperia pedunculata. This species is larger and sturdier than *C. drummondi,* and the flower tube is shorter.

CULTURE: The same as for amarcrinum, but start growth in a completely dark room. Apply manure water when buds begin to swell.

CRINUM

In spite of the fact that crinum has been recommended and praised in many garden books and catalogues, it is surprising how few gardeners can say honestly that they have grown and flowered any one of the numerous species and varieties. However, mention the name crinum to many indoor gardeners and they will tell you how to grow the plants, and which may be grown out of doors. In New England this may not be as anomalous as it sounds, for *Crinum moorei* has been grown there for decades in pots, pans, washtubs, and dooryard gardens.

There are over 100 recognized species in the genus, some of medium size and moderately hardy as garden plants. Others attain such large stature they outgrow facile handling under house or greenhouse culture. Certain members of the group, however, make good house plants, and undertake the project in a fragrant, enthusiastic manner. Flowers of most crinums are lily-shaped and are borne in umbels in typical amaryllis manner. Some of the plants flower once a season; others will blossom several times if dried off a little, then watered freely. Very large pots or tubs are necessary as containers for crinum bulbs and foliage. Newly planted bulbs sometimes are slow in producing flowers.

DESCRIPTION: *Crinum asiaticum.* Grows to 6 feet in height from a bulb-like root often 1 foot in length. Huge umbels of large white flowers, with long narrow petals, are produced. The leaves are long, thin, erect, and quite stiff. Winter is the flowering season. Called the poison bulb.

Crinum longifolium. Grows from a bulb. Often listed in catalogues as *Crinum capense alba* or *rosea,* as there are both white and pink forms. The leaves are long and narrow with rough margins. Flowers are lily-like, 8-12 in a cluster, and 2-4 inches wide. This South African crinum is probably the most widely grown member of the genus. The hardy crinum.

Crinum moorei. Grows from a bulb. Bell-shaped pink flowers about 4 inches across appear in the fall. Leaves are smooth and about 3 inches wide; length 2-3 feet. Long-neck crinum.

Crinum powelli. Grows from a bulb. This is a hybrid of *C. longifolium* x *C. moorei.* A splendid plant with deep green leaves up to 4 feet in length. 8-12 lily-like flowers are carried on 2-3 foot stalks. Varieties are obtainable in white, light pink, and deep rosy-pink.

Crinum, Cecil Houdyshel. Grows from a bulb. A hybrid of *C. longifolium* x *C. moorei.* The flowers are produced almost monthly. One of the best hybrids in cultivation.

Crinum, Ellen Bosanquet. A new hybrid with unusual flowers of burgundy-red.

Crinum, Gordon Wayne. Another large hybrid crinum with luxuriant foliage and brilliant white flowers. Dormant in midsummer, it grows actively the rest of the year.

As has been mentioned previously, there are many species and varieties of crinum known. Not all of them are in cultivation; yet a far greater number than have been described here are available. With subjects of large size, however, probably not more than one specimen will be grown in an indoor collection, unless a large area is available.

CULTURE: The culture of crinum is comparatively easy, as, once established, the plants will thrive under conditions which hint of neglect. Like other South African bulbs, crinum needs rest and ripening after flowering. Lay the containers on their sides for several months. If the dormant period is in the summer, store out of doors under a shrub; if winter resting is indicated store in a warm dry cellar. When brought into active growth again after a siesta, replace the top 2 inches of soil with fresh potting mixture (regular amaryllis potting soil). Additional plants may be obtained from small bulb offsets which root easily. Liquid fertilizer is helpful during the growing season, and a copious supply of water. Species and horticultural varieties with evergreen foliage should not be dried off entirely, yet watering may be reduced to a minimum during the resting period.

CURCULIGO

A small genus of amaryllids mostly from Asia and Australia. One cultivated species is grown in greenhouses, and may be grown in window gardens where a moist atmosphere and a temperature of about 75 degrees is available.

DESCRIPTION: *Curculigo capitulata* is a stemless herb producing a heavy growth of handsome foliage. The leaves are basal, 1-3 feet long, recurved, and plaited in an interesting manner. Yellow flowers, about ¾ of an inch wide, are carried on short stalks. Flower clusters are always near the ground and partly hidden by the leaves.

CULTURE: The same as for amarcrinum, but warmth and humidity are essential for proper cultivation. This is an excellent subject for those interested in rare house plants.

CYRTANTHUS

Commonly called the Ifafa lily, this South African amaryllid is a charming plant. The drooping tubular flowers are available in a number of colors. Strangely enough it seldom is grown in this country, although indoor gardeners in England and Europe know and appreciate it. There are both small and large-flowered species, and some fine hybrids. Most species in cultivation have persistent, strap-shaped leaves and typical amaryllis flower clusters atop sturdy hollow stalks. Cyrtanthus grows easily from purchased bulbs, also from seeds, if one is not too particular about having all the seed parent characteristics in seedling plants. The genus responds readily to house culture.

DESCRIPTION: *Cyrtanthus parviflorus.* Grows from a bulb. Narrow, limber leaves about 1 foot long. The flowers are red, ¾-1¼ inches in length, and 6-8 are produced in each umbel.

Cyrtanthus lutescens. Grows from a bulb. Leaves, 2-4 in number, are produced at the same time or after flowers have opened. The foliage is bright green, each leaf about 1 foot in length and limber. 2-3 yellowish flowers are carried on slender stalks which vary in height from 6-12 inches. Each bulb produces flowers over a long period.

Cyrtanthus mackeni. Grows from a bulb. Leaves are produced with the flowers. Blossoms are white, nearly erect, 2 inches long, and there are 4-10 in each cluster. The flower stalk is 12 inches high and quite reddish at the base.

C. carneus, C. flammeus, and *C. sanguineus* are three more members of the group whose brilliant red flowers are exemplified by the specific names accorded them.

Here again the list of available species and varieties has not been covered completely. Examination of catalogues from dealers who specialize in amaryllids will disclose other cyrtanthus worth growing in the window garden.

CULTURE: The potting mixture should consist of equal parts of peat moss, sharp sand, and rich loam. Water whenever necessary, but do not overdo it or a devastating rot will make its appearance. Cyrtanthus should be grown in a temperature not exceeding 65 degrees. 55-60 degrees is better still, for the plant requires cool growing conditions. After flowering, dry off gradually and ripen bulbs (still potted) in the sun. Then place containers on side in cellar for a rest period, bringing into active growth again when wanted.

ELISENA

Elisena longipetala is a recently introduced species from South America. I have had no personal experience with the plant; yet it sounds interesting and practical for use as a house plant. About it Mr. Cecil Houdyshel, the introducer, says; ". . . a very rare amaryllid from Peru. The bulb and plant closely resemble the Ismene (*Hymenocallis calathina*) and culture is the same. The flowers are much prettier than the common Ismene, being pure white with long graceful petals. Since it can be dug in the fall and stored it can be grown anywhere; but as it likes a long season we suggest starting it in pots."

CULTURE: The same as for hymenocallis, which see.

EUCHARIS

The amazon lily is a representative of the amaryllis family from South America. One species only is in general cultivation, *Eucharis grandiflora,* from Colombia and Brazil. The same plant is listed in many catalogues as *Eucharis amazonica.*

California and Florida gardeners find eucharis lovely as an outdoor plant; elsewhere it must be grown in the greenhouse or window garden.

DESCRIPTION: *Eucharis grandiflora.* Grows from a bulb. Leaves are 8-12 inches long, about one-half as wide, and carried on slender leafstalks. The fragrant flowers are pure white and funnel-shaped, 2-3 inches wide. Flowers are carried in clusters on 1-2 foot stalks. Spring is the usual blooming period, yet alternate drying and bringing into growth will usually produce several crops of flowers.

CULTURE: Eucharis is not as easy to bring into flower as other amaryllids. Often it is quite stubborn; yet when flowers are coaxed into being, their beauty justifies the effort and previous disappointments.

A warm humid atmosphere is the first requisite; and pot-bound roots are absolutely essential for blooming, so be sure to use small containers when planting. The potting mixture should consist of well decayed compost, peat, and ground limestone. Bone meal may be substituted for the limestone. A short rest period is advisable after flowering.

HAEMANTHUS

An extremely interesting amaryllid from South Africa bearing the sanguinary common name of blood lily: also it is called snakeshead lily. Huge globular clusters of flowers, surrounded by colorful bracts, are carried at the end of flower stalks. Haemanthus has been cultivated for more than a century in England; here it is practically unknown. The plants are most startling when seen in flower for the first time.

DESCRIPTION: *Haemanthus coccineus*. Grows from a bulb. The 2 leaves are tongue-shaped and fleshy, 1-2 feet long, and succulent in character. Flowers are bright red with yellow anthers, many in a globular umbel about 3 inches in diameter. The bracts are 6-8 inches in length and red in color.

Haemanthus katherinae. Grows from a bulb. Leaves are 9-12 inches in length and oblong in shape. They are produced at the same time as the flowers and number 3-5. The leaf-stalks are 4-6 inches long and spotted. Flowers are red to salmon, with yellow anthers. The flower cluster is longer than in the species above, sometimes reaching 10 inches in diameter and carried on a stalk about 1 foot in height.

Haemanthus multiflorus. One of the best species for use as a house plant. The umbels of brilliant red flowers sometimes exceed 1 foot in diameter on well established bulbs. *H. multiflorus* is quite different in appearance from *H. coccineus.* The bulb has a stem-like neck and the flowers appear in early spring before the leaves have grown. Use oakleaf mold in the potting mixture for best results.

CULTURE: Regular amaryllis potting mixture to which leaf mold or humus has been added. Provide additional drainage material. Cover the bulbs to one-half their depth. Little water is required until growth begins, and it should be withheld entirely when foliage starts to turn. Dry the bulbs in the sun for several weeks before resting. Use manure water throughout the growing season.

HYMENOCALLIS

The spider lilies are showy bulbous plants. About 40 of them are known, mostly from Tropical America. The genus is generally recognized for the lovely summer-flowering lily-basket, or ismene (*Hymenocallis calathina*), and its even more beautiful hybrids and varieties, Advance, Festalis, Olympic, and Sulphur Queen. A few wild species occur in the southwest, and from Carolina to Florida; yet they are seldom cultivated except in wild gardens. There is one winter-flowering species indigenous to Florida and the West Indies which is in cultivation. Because of its flowering season it makes a splendid house plant.

DESCRIPTION: *Hymenocallis caribaea.* Grows from a bulb with little or no neck. The leaves, from 12-20, vary 10-20 inches in length and usually are quite wide—about 3 inches.

Flowers are white, very fragrant, 4-6 inches long, and tubular for about one-half the length.

Three other species, available in the trade, which are worth a trial as pot plants are *Hymenocallis galvestonensis* and *Hymenocallis harrisiana,* and *Hymenocallis festalis.*

CULTURE: Use regular amaryllis potting mixture and cultivation. Rest the bulbs during July and August (*H. caribaea*).

LYCORIS

This Asiatic bulbous group of the amaryllis family embraces numerous exquisite plants, both hardy and tender in northern latitudes. The hardiest is the mystery lily, *Lycoris squamigera,* and its darker hued cousin, *Lycoris purpurea.* Both are sometimes catalogued and called Hall's amaryllis. These plants, which flower in the fall on naked stems, are of more interest in gardens than in the house. Other species and varieties are more satisfactory as greenhouse or window garden subjects; for definitely they are of questionable hardiness anywhere but in southern latitudes. The group as a whole sends up strap-like leaves which flourish and die down, later followed by sturdy stalks supporting clusters of typical amaryllis flowers; although certain of the species have blossoms which deviate from the tubular form and resemble the spidery outline of nerine flowers (which see at the next entry). All in all it is a splendid genus and has a lot to offer the curious gardener who will take the time and trouble to explore the possibilities of available lycoris. Mostly all species are fall-blooming.

DESCRIPTION: *Lycoris aurea.* Grows from a bulb. An exquisite golden form with flowers of the tubular type.

Lycoris incarnata. A pink-flowered lycoris. The tubular flowers are streaked with red and present a striking appearance.

Lycoris radiata. Quite often this plant is called, incorrectly, *Nerine sarniensis.* There is a plant which is described in the next entry that bears the name correctly. As you might expect, flowers of the two species have much in common. The red, spidery-looking blossoms of both are particularly fine and desirable on a house plant.

CULTURE: Use regular amaryllis potting mixture, with the addition of 25% more sand. Handle in the manner prescribed for hymenocallis (regular amaryllis culture).

NERINE

The Guernsey lily, as nerine is called, deserves wide recognition and use as a house plant. Few flowers equal those to be found in this genus for brilliancy and remarkable texture. Truly, here is a flower sprinkled with stardust; for the texture is such that light is reflected as though from innumerable small facets or mirrors. The effect is that of scintillating, powdered gold.

In some species leaves follow the flowers; in others, foliage is produced before, or simultaneously with, blossoms. October to January is the usual flowering period, which makes nerine ideal for early winter color. While all amaryllids are noted for the beauty of their flowers, few members of the family can compete with nerine in sheer charm.

Species described in the following paragraphs are available from numerous sources in the United States. They represent but a small section of known species not in cultivation. If indoor gardeners will grow this fine amaryllid in sufficient numbers, the trade will be glad to stock and sell a larger group of nerines.

DESCRIPTION: *Nerine sarniensis.* This is the true Guernsey lily. Grows from a bulb. The leaves are nearly erect, narrow, and bright green in color. They are about ¾ inch wide and 12-18 inches in length. The flower cluster is carried upon a slender stalk, and is composed of 8-24 spidery, crimson flowers.

Nerine curvifolia. Not yet available here, as far as I know, but scheduled to be offered soon. Similar in many respects to *N. sarniensis,* but leaves appear after the flowers and are of thicker substance. Fewer individual blossoms are produced in each umbel, and they are brilliant scarlet in color. Watch for this species in dealers' catalogues, and its varieties, *fothergilli,* and *fothergilli major.*

Nerine filifolia. Near the top of the list of desirable species. Leaves and flowers are produced at the same time. The leaves are small and grass-like, 5-8 inches long, often with a downy bloom. 8-12 flowers occur in each umbel, each blossom of glowing red.

Several growers offer hybrid nerines, too, many of which have superior characteristics.

CULTURE: Use regular amaryllis potting mixture. Note that nerines demand a long rest after the leaves have dried off. Neglect in attending to this detail has accounted for much

of the difficulty in getting satisfactory results after first flowering. A few nerines have evergreen foliage. These, of
course, should never be dried off completely. The others re-
quest a resting spot in a sunny cellar window. Leave the pot
upright and cover the yellowed leaves with a handful of
marsh hay. After at least ninety days' rest, begin to water
the plants again and increase moisture gradually as new
growth becomes evident. Nerines are particularly grateful
for repeated applications of manure water during the growing season.

Some authorities recommend that the bulbs be depotted in
June or July and stored until late autumn, then replanted.
Yet, recognizing the reluctance of the entire amaryllis family
to root-disturbance, I have always considered it safer to leave
bulbs in the containers just as long as possible.

PANCRATIUM

PANCRATIUM

A little known group of bulbous Asiatic plants. The genus
comprises about 14 species, yet one only is in general cultivation.

Pancratium maritimum. It grows from a long-necked, globular bulb which produces bluish-green leaves 2 feet in length. The flower stalk is heavy, somewhat flattened, and carries an umbel of 5-10 fragrant, lily-like white flowers.

CULTURE: Use regular amaryllis potting mixture and handle like amarcrinum.

SPREKELIA

A genus of the amaryllis family which boasts of one species only, *Sprekelia formosissima,* a native of Mexico; called there amacayo, and here known colloquially as Jacobean or St. James lily. Occasionally it will be found in catalogues under *Amaryllis formosissima.*

DESCRIPTION: *Sprekelia formosissima.* Grows from an ovalish bulb. The leaves are few in number, narrow, thick, and 8-12 inches long. The solitary red flower is carried—before the leaves appear—on stalks about 1 foot tall. Flowers are 4 inches long and each is enclosed in a membranaceous spathe.

CULTURE: Regular amaryllis potting mixture. Handle like amarcrinum. Sprekelia also may be flowered in pebbles and water like paper-white narcissus. If this method of growing is used, however, the bulbs are of no further use as ripening is incomplete.

VALLOTA

We can thank South Africa for this lovely amaryllid. It is a favorite house plant abroad; in the United States it is grown sparingly as a garden plant in California. Elsewhere its use here for any purpose is very limited. For many reasons it should be included in the window garden collection. The large, scarlet to dark red, tubular flowers are magnificent. First blooming often is slow and irregular, yet once the plant has flowered it will continue to do so with punctuality. Flowering period is from mid-summer until fall.

DESCRIPTION: *Vallota purpurea.* The strap-shaped leaves appear after the flowers, and are 1-2 feet in length; width, about 1¼ inches. The flower stalk is tall, 2-3 feet, and carries 5-10 bright scarlet flowers at the apex. Flower tubes have a greenish cast. Commonly called Scarboro lily.

Vallota magnifica. A horticultural variety with 4 inch scarlet flowers, each with a white eye. Otherwise similar to *V. purpurea.*

CULTURE: The best potting mixture for vallota consists of equal parts of rich fibrous loam, leaf mold, peat, and sharp sand. Place bulb points just below the soil surface and pot them in May. Rest after flowering, as with other amaryllids, yet do not withhold water entirely; supply enough to prevent complete drying off. Do not disturb the planting until absolutely necessary, but dig in an inch of fresh soil after each resting period.

This completes entries under the amaryllis family. It does not represent a complete listing, of course, either of common species or plants not in cultivation.

III

ARUM FAMILY

.

Chapter 3

ARUM FAMILY

AN IMMENSE FAMILY of plants which collectively are
spoken of as aroids. Most members of this group are tender
tropical herbs: a few hardy representatives, like jack-in-the-
pulpit, *Calla palustris,* and skunk cabbage, are native to the
United States. Otherwise, any window garden collection of
aroids represents an international selection of subjects.

All aroids share one thing in common, the type of flowers
produced. They are small, insignificant, and borne on an
appendage called a spadix which arises from a sheath-like
structure known as a spathe. In many instances, such as calla
and anthurium, the spathe is lovely in shape and color and is
thought of as the flower. Actually, apetalous true flowers are
clustered on the spadix; pollen-bearing male flowers on the
upper part, and female flowers below. Size, shape, color, and
mutual arrangement of spathe and spadix vary in different
species; yet essentially are the same throughout the entire
group.

The arum family comprises over 100 genera and about
1500 species of plants. As you would expect, there is a wide
difference in sizes. The familiar Chinese evergreen, aglaon-

THE GIANT CALLA (*Amorphophallus titanum*)

ema, produces spathes little more than 1 inch in length; while a Sumatran aroid, *Amorphophallus titanum,* erects a spadix 6 feet in length, enveloped by a fringed spathe 3-4 feet in diameter.

Another characteristic of the arum family, which must be taken into consideration when selecting specimens for growing indoors, is the charnel house odor which clings to certain species. Skunk cabbage is a familiar example. When a specimen of *A. titanum,* mentioned above, was flowered in the Brooklyn Botanic greenhouse several years ago, gas masks were used! Fortunately this skatolic breath contaminates but few aroids; there is no hint of it in many of the most beautiful.

Members of the arum family are used in tropical and subtropical plantings, a few in the wild garden; but mostly they find primary use as house or greenhouse specimens, in which category they are deservedly popular.

Warmth and humidity are essential in the cultivation of most aroids. If this can be provided the plants may be grown with little effort. Aroids are lovers of water, many growing naturally in damp places. Several species, including Chinese evergreen and philodendron, will grow directly in water without need of potting soil; although the same plants will do better when potted.

For general use with Araceae, the following potting mixture will be found beneficial. Two parts good loam; two parts leaf mold; two parts dried cow manure; one-half part sharp sand; one-eighth part bone meal. Any exceptions will be noted under individual plant entries.

Inasmuch as most of the aroids to be described require

abundant watering but not permanent sogginess, be sure to provide plenty of drainage material in the containers before planting; and watch saucers and supplementary bowls for standing water.

ALOCASIA

A large genus of plants, Araceae, native to Asia and the Malayan Islands. Comparatively few species and varieties are in cultivation. Those that are available are grown for the striking leaves which usually are mottled and colored, sometimes with a distinct metallic sheen that is lovely under artificial light.

DESCRIPTION: *Alocasia indica,* var. *metallica.* Grows from a heavy rootstock. Leaves are 2-4 feet long, arrow-shaped, with a red-purple sheen. The spathe is boat-shaped, pale yellow outside and often is red inside.

Alocasia indica, var. *variegata.* Similar to above plant but the leaves are green, mottled with silver.

Alocasia sanderiana. A species from the Philippine Islands, smaller than the *Alocasia indica* varieties. Leaves are triangular and about 1 foot long. The upper surface is dark green, veined and margined with white; the lower surface is purplish. Spathe is green and of little decorative value.

CULTURE: Regular arum potting mixture. The temperature in winter should never be below 65 degrees, and 70 degrees is to be preferred, together with a moist atmosphere. Plant the rootstock several inches below the surface of the soil, and feed monthly with manure water. Water freely and often. Older plants of *Alocasia indica* varieties will in time have to be grown in tubs, for the stems eventually attain 6 feet in height and the plant assumes corresponding proportions.

ANTHURIUM

One of the largest genera in the arum family, including climbers as well as herbs. One or two species may be found at many florists' and greenhouses, yet it is surprising how few window gardens contain a specimen. Probably the best known species is the flamingo flower, *Anthurium scherzerianum,* and its numerous horticultural varieties with spathes of white, yellow, pink, or red. Other anthuriums are grown for the decorative foliage, as spathes in a few species are nondescript. It is a fine group and deserves wide use. The flowering period is in late winter and early spring.

DESCRIPTION: *Anthurium andraeanum.* A South American species with 12 inch, heart-shaped leaves about one-half as wide as they are long. The spathe is 6 inches in length, leathery in texture, and colored a brilliant orange.

Anthurium scherzerianum. Leaves are 8 inches long, and 2 inches wide, green, and narrowing at the end to a fine tip. The spadix is yellow and coiled. Spathes, as mentioned previously, are variously colored. All are about 3 inches in length.

Anthurium veitchi. A species from South America grown for its foliage. The oblong leaves are 3 feet in length and about 10 inches wide. They are of metallic-green with prominent veins on the under surface. Recently, interior decorators have made considerable use of the plant.

CULTURE: Regular arum potting mixture, to which add two

parts of either osmunda or sphagnum moss for increased humus content. Keep the plants out of direct sun and spray each week until flower buds are formed. Then water from the bottom as the spathes are badly spotted by drops of water. Humidity is helpful and the growing temperature should not drop below 65 degrees. Established plants seldom require repotting, yet do welcome an inch of new potting soil yearly.

ARUM

A group of Eurasian aroids related to jack-in-the-pulpit. With few exceptions, of no particular interest as house plants. One of the exceptions is *Arum palaestinum,* called black calla and Solomon's lily, also *Arum sanctum.* This species is extremely interesting and well merits a place in the window garden collection. It grows from a tuberous root. The arrow-shaped leaves are most decorative. Spathes resemble those of calla lilies but are green outside and purple-black within.

The other house plant arum is *Arum italicum.* It grows from a thick rootstock and is not unlike jack-in-the-pulpit. The spathes are white or greenish-yellow and appear in early spring. Handsome scarlet berries are borne, after the flowers, on naked, 8-10 inch stems. Large arrow-shaped leaves of shining texture are produced in the fall and remain green over winter in outside plantings. A variety, *marmoratum,* has variegated leaves mottled with yellow.

CULTURE: Start tubers in damp chopped moss, covering them about 2 inches. When roots have formed pot the tubers in individual containers just big enough to accommodate each tuber. Use a potting mixture consisting of one part loam; one part leaf mold; and one part sand. When plants have outgrown original pots, transplant into new containers filled with regular arum potting mixture. Keep the new pots relatively small, however, for the plants flower better when partly rootbound. Grow in a temperature of 70-75 degrees and water abundantly.

Proper cultivation demands ample light; yet torrid, direct sun rays will burn leaves and spathes. In greenhouses this condition is treated by whitewashing the glass. Window gardeners may accomplish the same result by using paper or curtains as a screen.

HYDROSME

A group of tropical bulbous herbs, evil-smelling, and lacking entirely in beauty; although certain of them are grown as curiosities. One in particular is offered by numerous dealers under the various names of *Amorphophallus rivieri*, devil's tongue, snake palm, and lily-of-India. Call the plant as you choose, the botanical name is *Hydrosme rivieri*.

It grows from a huge bulbous rootstock which sends forth a dark red, calla-like spathe that is carried on a fleshy, spotted stalk 2-4 feet high. Leaves appear after the spathe and spadix have wilted. They are not unattractive, being about 4 feet in width, divided and re-divided, somewhat palm-like in appearance.

CULTURE: Use regular arum potting mixture and plant the latter part of March. Rest over winter in a cool place, 50 degrees, and reduce watering. Rootstocks 3-5 years old are required for flowering.

Monstera

A small tropical genus. Few of the 50 known species are in cultivation. One climbing species is grown in the north for its remarkable leaves, and in the south for the delicately flavored fruit. It is the ceriman, *Monstera deliciosa*. Old plants attain a size which makes their use impractical in the average indoor garden, yet younger plants provide excellent specimens for the purpose.

In the native habitat most members of the genus grow as epiphytes, attached to tree trunks far above the ground. Long aerial roots, to absorb moisture and gasses from the air, are produced. Indians dry these roots and employ them in the manufacture of strong, pliable baskets. Often the roots exceed 20 feet in length.

The plants will climb in the house or greenhouse if given suitable support. Also, lacking support, monstera seems perfectly happy to remain a bush-like, spreading plant, in which condition it flowers more readily than when trained in vine form.

The ceriman frequently produces fruit under greenhouse culture; seldom in the house.

CULTURE: Use regular arum potting mixture and supply a strong support for the plant. Water frequently and supply as warm and humid location as is practical. While the plant will benefit from a short rest, usually it is kept in continuous active growth.

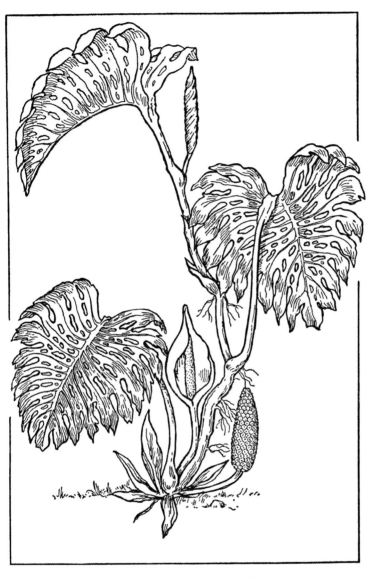

THE CERIMAN *(Monstera deliciosa)*
Illustrating fruit, spathe and spadix, and bud

PHILODENDRON

Handsome climbing aroids of Tropical America. In the wild, some philodendrons grow to great heights; others are tree-perching. As house plants they make fine foliage specimens and seldom get out of hand, although they do appreciate ample growing space.

To most indoor gardeners the name philodendron connotes the rugged little species sold by most florists as *Philodendron cordatum*. It persists under the most adverse growing conditions and will bring living green to many dark corners.

In addition to this familiar vine, the genus offers other species of greater size and flamboyancy. They are little known; nevertheless they are worthy subjects for the window garden and give of their beauty generously with moderate care and attention; although they will not survive the indifferent treatment usually accorded *Philodendron cordatum*.

DESCRIPTION: *Philodendron devansayeanum*. A species from Peru with long-pointed, heart-shaped leaves 10-20 inches in length. The foliage on young plants is reddish, changing to green as the plants mature. The white spathe is about 6 inches long. The plant grows from a thick rootstock.

Philodendron verrucosum. This climber has oval or heart-shaped leaves deeply split at the base. They are green above and lined with salmon on the under side. Leafstalks are red in color and hairy. Leaves are 8 inches long and 6 inches wide. The boat-shaped spathe is purplish.

Spathe and Spadix of *Monstera deliciosa*. Page 64

Syngonium podophyllum. Page 71

Syngonium podophyllum, var. Ruth Fraser. Page 71

Syngonium podophyllum, var. Dot Mae. Page 71

Xanthosoma lindeni. Page 72

CULTURE: Regular arum potting mixture, to which add two parts of orchid fiber (osmunda). The two species described above are excellent for locations in north windows as they require but little sun. Water copiously and supply ample drainage material. No resting necessary. Warmth and a moist atmosphere will produce healthier, larger specimens. Supply a support for the plants.

SAUROMATUM

SAUROMATUM

Queer aroids from India, Java, and Tropical Africa, related to arisaema and hydrosme. The genus derives its name from *saura,* lizard; referring to the spotted spathes. About 6 species are known, 3 of which are in cultivation; all from the Himalayas. They are moderately hardy, but are best used as house plants, in which capacity they make weird and unusual specimens.

DESCRIPTION: *Sauromatum guttatum.* Grows from a large, tuberous rootstock. From the form of the spathe, pig's tail calla would seem to be an appropriate common name for the plant. The large spathe is dull ivory in color, tinted with rose, and lined with purple. The top of the spathe-blade bends over and trails to the ground in a series of diminishing spirals; the effect is startling.

Sauromatum nubicum. Possibly a variety of *S. guttatum,* yet for the present it is accorded specific rank. The only difference between the two plants is in the color of the spathe. In *S. nubicum* it is dark red with yellow markings.   ·

Sauromatum venosum. Grows from a tuberous rootstock. This lizard lily leaves much to be desired in the way of fragrance, yet it is a curious and interesting plant to grow. The unique spathe is 14-16 inches long, 1 inch broad, and is colored yellow with purple-black spots. The colloquial name of this sauromatum was suggested by the fact that the long slender spathe lies on the ground instead of growing in an upright position.

CULTURE: In February, the pouch-like rootstocks may be placed in a window where there is good light but little sun. It is not necessary to plant the rootstock; just rest it in a saucer or plate. Rapidly the spathe will appear, develop, and wilt. When warm weather permits, plant the rootstock in the outdoor garden; it will produce an exotic leaf growth. Dig and rest the rootstock from September until February.

SCHISMATOGLOTTIS

Tender aroids, native to the Malayan Islands, which rarely are grown here. There are some 75 recognized species; one only is in cultivation, *Schismatoglottis picta;* a splendid, but very tender foliage plant which requires a growing temperature of at least 70 degrees. It grows from a thick rootstock. Leaves are oval in shape, about 8 inches long, colored light green, and spotted with white. The small spathe is greenish-yellow and nearly 3 inches long.

CULTURE: Regular arum potting mixture. Rest as you would calla lilies after flowering. Maintenance of even, moist heat is essential, and use care when airing out the room wherein the plant is growing; for a touch of really cold air is fatal to this immigrant from Java.

SCINDAPSUS

A group of aroid climbers from Malaya. Available plants in the trade also are known as pothos; particularly the ivy arum which is called *Pothos aureus*. The two species described may be used as vines or as trailing plants in hanging pots.

DESCRIPTION: *Scindapsus aureus (Pothos aureus)*. In time the ivy arum will grow to a considerable height. The broad, lance-shaped leaves are sometimes lobed, sometimes not. They are spotted with yellow, 16-18 inches long, and 10-12 inches wide. The plant grows from a rootstock.

Scindapsus pictus, var. *argyraeus.* A tall climber with 6 inch, heart-shaped leaves marked on the under side with silvery spots. Both species produce white spathes, although they seldom appear on specimens grown as house plants.

CULTURE: Potting soil for scindapsus should consist of equal parts of peat (not peat moss), osmunda fiber, and sand. Include some charcoal. Provide light but little sun (1-2 hours daily). No resting period required.

SPATHIPHYLLUM

A Tropical American genus which is nearly as rare in cultivation as schismatoglottis. Recently, however, several species have been used in arrangements at flower shows with enthusiastic success.

DESCRIPTION: *Spathiphyllum floribundum*. Grows from a fleshy rootstock. The sheathed leafstalks are about 6 inches in length; leaves are 6 inches long and a little over 2 inches in width. One-half of the leaf is larger than the other, and the upper side is darker than the lower. The spathe is white and 1½-2½ inches long.

Spathiphyllum patini. Similar to the above species but larger in all its parts.

CULTURE: Regular arum potting mixture. Grow at a temperature of 65-70 degrees and water abundantly. Keep the plants a little rootbound and give manure water occasionally. Rest by reducing the water supply, but not the temperature. Pots containing spathiphyllum may be plunged outdoors in the garden in July and August. They should be returned to the house before there is any chance of frost striking.

SYNGONIUM

Seldom-grown, Tropical American plants of the arum family. About 10 species are known. All are woody climbing or creeping plants with acrid milky sap. When young, the plants show little or no climbing tendency; this develops later. The handsome, arrow-shaped leaves are carried on long, sheathed leafstalks. As they grow older, the leaves become divided into 5-9 parts and are very striking in appearance. Flower stalks are short and carry small spathes of yellowish or whitish-green. Spadix is shorter than the spathe. Several varieties are used as house plants for the decorative foliage and tropical appearance.

DESCRIPTION: *Syngonium podophyllum*. Leaves are 4-6 inches long; leafstalks 15-20 inches in length. The spathe is about 2½ inches long, greenish outside, white within.

Syngonium podophyllum, var. *albolineatum*. Similar to above species, but the leaves are ribbed boldly in white.

Mr. Carl Fraser of Bradenton, Florida, has developed several sports of *S. podophyllum* which have distinctive, variegated leaves of great beauty. Three of Mr. Fraser's introductions are:

Syngonium podophyllum, var. Daphne. The leaf variegation is creamy-white and occupies most of the leaf area.

Syngonium podophyllum, var. Ruth Fraser. In this sport, most of the leaves are smaller and more graceful than in the type. The variegation is white and covers 80-90 percent of each leaf.

Syngonium podophyllum, var. Dot Mae. The leaves in this variety are wider than in the type, and leaf division does not take place as early in the plant's life. Extensive white variegation.

CULTURE: Syngonium is a very tender aroid and revels in

heat and humidity. Use regular arum potting mixture; and if you wish to develop the plant as a climber, supply a suitable support. No resting necessary.

XANTHOSOMA

Another Tropical American genus of the arum family, grown in the south for the edible rootstocks, and in the north as ornamental plants. Several species have truly beautiful foliage, and all bear spathes from 4-12 inches long depending upon the species. Plants in this group, which are suitable for pot subjects, are very satisfactory.

DESCRIPTION: *Xanthosoma lindeni.* Leaves are 12 inches long, 4-6 inches wide, and numerous. Leafblades are veined heavily in white. Leafstalks up to 12 inches. The white spathe is 4-6 inches in length.

Xanthosoma violaceum. A larger plant than *X. lindeni,* with leaves veined in purple instead of white. The yellowish-white spathes are nearly a foot in length.

CULTURE: The same as for caladium and *Arum palaestinum.*

The list of available aroids is not long. Of the 100 genera included under Araceae, very few are offered for sale.

No mention has been made of common species. Such plants, for instance, as aglaonema and dieffenbachia. Nor has zantedeschia, the calla lily group, been discussed as it is too widely grown to be included in a book of this character and intent. Yet I have been tempted to include the callas, for there are varieties now available that are superior in every way to the familiar white and yellow callas. If you are interested in these plants it will pay to examine the new catalogues.

2 parts loam
2 parts leaf mold
2 parts dried cow manure
½ part sand
⅛ part bone meal

ARUM POTTING MIXTURE

IV

IRIS FAMILY

Chapter 4

IRIS FAMILY

W<small>HILE</small> the number of genera and species included in the Iridaceae is not as large as those to be found in the arum family, for practical purposes it is a much greater family, as most members of the group are in cultivation and plants of importance.

One of the irid divisions contains such beloved and familiar plants as belamcanda, crocus, gladiolus, iris, tigridia, and tritonia. These, for the most part, are plants for the outdoor garden, although many of them are grown in the house, too. With a few exceptions they will not be mentioned here, because there are so many other lovely and unusual irids that are too tender to grow out of doors in northern latitudes, yet may be enjoyed in window gardens everywhere.

Members of the iris family grow from bulbs, corms, or rhizomes; a few have fibrous roots for underground parts. Flowers in many genera are tubular; others, as in iris and morea, have expanded stigmas which give the impression of flowers with separate petals. Many are fragrant, some intensely so—freesia, for instance, and the little species glad-

77

iolus, *Gladiolus tristis*. Colors of great brilliancy, too, are associated with the Iridaceae.

The group as a whole is quite amenable to house culture, and has the attribute of providing plants which flower at different seasons; thus affording a succession of bloom. Also there is a much greater variance in sizes, shapes, and colors than is found in many plant families.

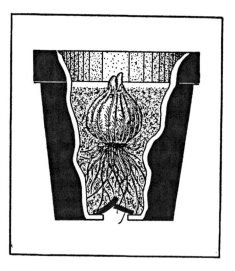

FIG. 2.   HEAVY ROOTING OF HARDY BULBS IS NECESSARY

Some of the irids to be described are hardy or semi-hardy in character; others are tender. Two growing methods must be observed. Hardy and semi-hardy bulbous irids will require a rooting period before top-growth is started. The tender species, in most instances, may be started into growth as soon as potted.

And here is another point to keep in mind. Many of the

most desirable irids for indoor culture grow from corms. Corms, as opposed to most true bulbs, do not persist in the ground for years; but exist for just one growing season. A new corm or corms are formed annually to replace the old corm which withers away. Undoubtedly you have noticed the desiccated, wrinkled old corm attached at the base of a plump new growth when you have lifted gladioli in the fall for winter storage.

Cormous plants grown in pots sometimes produce new corms of flowering size; sometimes they do not. Instead of one or two large new corms, it is not unusual to find a number of small cormels which must be grown on for another year or two before they attain ability to send up flower stalks. Culture and available soil food has, of course, a definite bearing on the production of new corms.

While it is instructive, interesting, and often practical to grow cormous plants so they will reproduce satisfactorily, the provident gardener will purchase and plant a few new corms each year to prevent disappointment.

Small corms and cormels, however, may be planted in the outdoor garden during the summer months, where some of them will increase to blooming size. They may then be lifted before frost makes its appearance, stored a while for drying and ripening, and potted for indoor forcing.

Members of the Iridaceae which grow from true bulbs, rhizomes, and fibrous roots will require different forcing treatment. Individual culture will be noted under each entry.

Unless otherwise designated, the general potting mixture for plants in this chapter is composed of: two parts rich

loam; two parts sharp sand; one-eighth part bone meal. Instructions for drainage strata obtain here as elsewhere.

ACIDANTHERA

This irid, indigenous to Abyssinia, was a favorite years
ago, then fell into disrepute. Today it is again assuming im-

2 parts rich loam
2 parts sharp sand
⅛ part bone meal

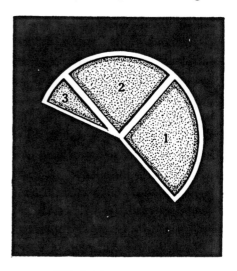

IRID POTTING MIXTURE

portance, and has numerous qualities which make it valuable
as a house plant. Although nearly 20 species are known,
just one is in general cultivation. It has a flowering schedule
of mid-to-late summer.

DESCRIPTION: *Acidanthera bicolor.* Grows from a small
brown corm which produces 1 or 2 sword-shaped leaves.
The flowers usually are creamy-white with chocolate
splotches at the base of each petal. They are about 4 inches

in length. Individual flowers are tubular in shape, some-what pendulous, and borne in a sparse cluster atop leafy, 18 inch stalks.

CULTURE: Use regular irid potting mixture. Plant the corms 2 inches deep and 6 inches apart in January, February, or March. Keep in a cool (50 degrees) dark place for several weeks; then bring into light for growing. A cool location where the temperature does not exceed 62 degrees produces the best flowers. After blooming, newly formed corms may be depotted and stored, but usually are not large enough to produce flowers the first season after planting. Better plant new corms each year.

While tender, acidanthera may be grown in the outdoor garden as well as indoors. Treat it exactly as you would gladiolus. Plantings should be made in June, and corms dug and stored over winter in the cellar.

ANTHOLYZA

African irids somewhat similar in appearance to gladiolus, but the flower tubes are longer and more slender. Of the numerous known species, 2 are available for house culture. Winter-blooming.

DESCRIPTION: *Antholyza aethiopica.* Grows from a corm. The narrow leaves are 16-20 inches long, typically iris-like in appearance. 2 inch, reddish-yellow flowers are clustered closely on spikes 6-10 inches long. The variety, Lucidor, has flowers of deep red and fascinating pink seed pods.

Antholyza paniculata. Grows from a large corm. Leaves are similar to above species but 3 inches wide instead of 1 inch. The wavy, 12 inch stalk carries numerous reddish-yellow flowers with curved tubes 1-1½ inches long.

CULTURE: Same as for acidanthera, but plant late in the summer. With adequate feeding and watering, new corms, large enough for the next year's forcing, are produced quite regularly.

ARISTEA

Aristea is a South African irid much beloved in its native country for the exquisite shades of blue that characterize the flowers of many species.

DESCRIPTION: *Aristea capitata.* Produces a basal cluster or rosette of rigid, linear leaves, 2-4 feet long, and about ½ inch wide. The flower stalks are 3-4 feet high bearing numerous panicles of brilliant blue flowers which are subtended by ½ inch membranaceous spathe-valves. A magnificent plant with a long period of bloom.

Aristea eckloni. Grows from an underground stem which produces basal rosettes of evergreen, 2-ranked leaves that are most decorative. The small, starry flowers are bright blue, and are borne in branching sprays on 12 inch, flattened stalks.

CULTURE: Plant the roots in a potting mixture consisting of: two parts loam; two parts leaf mold or humus; one part sand; one-half part dried cow manure. Grow in good light without direct sun, and water frequently. Retain but a few of the numerous flower stalks on the plant or leaves only will be produced. Pot in late fall or early winter. As the plant is evergreen do not dry off entirely; just reduce watering to allow the plant a brief rest before again undertaking the production of flowers.

BABIANA

The baboon flower also comes from South Africa, where its bright colors and interesting plaited leaves are familiar sights. Here, however, it is necessary to grow a few corms

BABIANA

in the house to enjoy babiana. This irid grows easily and quickly from seed, if you can acquire any. If not, corms of several species and horticultural varieties are available at very modest prices. Spring-flowering.

DESCRIPTION: *Babiana plicata.* Grows from a corm. Hairy, stemmed leaves, 5-6, with a narrow blade 3-6 inches long. The leafstalks are 4-6 inches in length. Lavender-blue flowers with creamy-white, crimson-flecked throats are borne in simple or forked spikes on hairy stalks. The fragrant flowers open wide.

Babiana stricta, var. *rubro-cyanea.* One of the loveliest babianas. Similar to the above species, but the flowers are of intense deep blue with centers of gleaming crimson. The plant is a little larger than *B. plicata,* growing to 8 inches.

Babiana sulphurea. An early-blooming species (February to March), with spicy-scented flowers of yellow and cream. Height, 12 inches.

Babiana, hybrids. A group of late spring-blooming plants with flowers in variant shades of pink, red, and blue. The hybrids are of easy culture and definite charm.

CULTURE: Regular irid potting mixture. Plant corms in late August or September, 1 inch deep, 12 to a 6 inch pot. Sink the pots out of doors without covering. Give very little water until growth is several inches high; then bring into the house. Grow in a cool, well-ventilated room and water frequently until flower buds have shown color. In fact, the soil in which babianas are growing never should be allowed to become dry.

After flowering, if the corms are as large, or nearly as large, as those originally planted, remove them from the pot and store away until the following summer.

CLEANTHE

This South African irid is not yet available, as far as I know. Somewhat like the morea tribe in appearance, it is too desirable as a house plant to remain forever as a wildling or specimen in a botanical garden. Sooner or later some grower will make members of the genus available to adventurous gardeners and reap a rich reward; for the plants will be purchased in quantity and grown widely.

The species, *Cleanthe bicolor,* resembles a small dainty iris on a wiry stem; with 3 segments of clear light blue, and 3 of almost pure black.

CROCOSMIA

A genus containing one South African herb of the iris family. This plant was one parent of the familiar garden montbretia. It is grown sparingly in the outdoor garden, and is of value for indoor culture.

DESCRIPTION: *Crocosmia aurea.* Grows from a small corm. Produces but few sword-shaped leaves, the lower ones shorter than those higher on the plant. The flowers are brilliant yellow-orange; the tube about 1 inch long, the segments longer and spreading. Blossoms are borne on spikes which may be either single or branching.

CULTURE: The same as for acidanthera, which see.

CYPELLA

South American irids related to tigridia, and commonly called shell flowers, due to shape and coloring. Leaves in this genus are interesting, being long and pleated. Spring to autumn-blooming. Other quite similar irids, also called shell flowers, are to be found in the genera *Eustylis* and *Hexaglottis*.

DESCRIPTION: *Cypella herberti.* Grows from a bulb. The large, buff-yellow flowers are carried on 2 foot stalks. Blooms continuously from early spring until late fall. Argentina is the habitat.

Cypella platensis. Similar to, and often called, the blue tigridia. The silk-like, bright blue flowers are carried on stalks about 3 feet in height. Blossoms are fugacious, lasting for a few hours only, although many are borne in succession.

Cypella plumbea. Very much like *C. platensis,* but the flowers are lead-colored, splayed with yellow in the center.

CULTURE: The same as for acidanthera, but the bulbs may be grown from year to year.

DIERAMA

Plants of the South African irid group which bear bell-shaped flowers on long thin stems. Colloquially they are called wedding or mountain bells. Both available species are beautiful and revel in damp treatment. Early spring-flowering.

DESCRIPTION: *Dierama pendula.* Grows from a small corm. The leaves are mostly basal, 12-20 inches long, and very narrow (¼ inch). Flowers are white to lavender in color, about 1 inch long, and borne in slender pendulous clusters nearly 4 feet in height.

Dierama pulcherrima. Catalogued also as *Sparaxis pulcherrima.* Grows from a corm. Similar to above species, but the flowers are a little larger (1½ inches) and are red-purple in color.

CULTURE: Use regular irid potting mixture. Plant the corms 1 inch deep, 8 to a 6 inch pot, in the fall. Keep pots in cold frame or covered in the cellar for 4-6 weeks until corms are well rooted. Then bring inside for growing. After top-growth is flourishing, water frequently and use manure water monthly. Plant new corms annually for best bloom.

FERRARIA

A small genus of irids from the Cape of Good Hope region containing 7 species, one of which is available in the United States. It is likely that the other species are just as interesting, perhaps more so, but they are not in cultivation. Plants in this group rarely exceed 6-10 inches in height. The foliage is very glaucous, lower leaves being long and linear; the rest are ovate, successively smaller, and topped by inflated sheaths from which the flowers appear. Each spathe contains several flowers which are united at the base. Blossoms are fugacious, lasting for one day or less, yet a number are borne in succession. Summer-blooming.

DESCRIPTION: *Ferraria undulata.* Grows from a large irregular corm. The 2 inch flowers are very odd. They consist of 6 spreading, triangular, petal-like lobes with frilled edges. The color is brownish-purple, edged with olive-green.

CULTURE: Plant in regular irid potting mixture, 2 or 3 corms to an 8 inch pot. Late winter or early spring is the planting time. Keep in a cool dark place for several weeks and give very little water. Then bring into the light, water freely, and place in the sun. After flowering, reduce water after the leaves have started to turn, ripen in the sun, and rest. It is preferable to remove the new corms from the pot, after ripening, and store them in peat moss.

GEISSORHIZA

A small group of charming little South African irids with brilliant, freesia-like flowers that appear in late summer on

ings made before January result in a large percentage of blind plants which are a disappointment always.

Plant corms 2 inches deep and 6 inches apart each way in regular irid potting mixture. Grow where you can maintain a day temperature of about 60 degrees, and a night temperature of 50 degrees. After flowering, discard the corms and purchase new ones the following year.

Hesperantha

Cormous plants of the iris family from the Cape of Good Hope region. About 28 species are recognized, several of which are in cultivation and available in the United States. Hesperanthae are related to the ixias, and are even more closely allied to geissorhiza. To be technical for a moment, the difference between hesperantha and geissorhiza lies in the fact that the former has longer style-branches, and the spathe-valves are green always instead of being brownish.

Leaves in this genus are 2-5. The flowers vary from 2-10 in number and are arranged in vertical rows on each side of the flower stalk. Mostly, the flowers have white inner segments, and outer segments red on the exterior, white inside.

The corms are quite small, seldom exceeding ½ inch in diameter.

DESCRIPTION: *Hesperantha falcata.* Grows from a conical corm. There are 2-4 lance-shaped leaves. The flowers are white inside, red on the exterior.

Hesperantha graminifolia. Grows from a small globular corm. The leaves are linear, 3-5 in number. Outer segments of the flowers are reddish-brown.

Hesperantha pilosa. Grows from a globular corm which produces 2 erect, linear leaves that are stiff and ribbed, each from 3-6 inches in length. The flowers are white inside, claret-red outside.

CULTURE: The same as for ixia, which see.

HOMERIA

HOMERIA

South African cormous plants related to gladiolus. In the natural habitat they are beautiful but poisonous weeds. They do, however, make splendid house plants; and the indoor gardener need have no qualms about toxic qualities of the plant, for it is unlikely that he will eat the specimen. Summer-blooming.

DESCRIPTION: *Homeria collina.* Grows from a corm. A single leaf is produced; a long, slender, strongly ribbed one that usually arches over and touches the ground at the tip. Flowers are borne in clusters on 1-1½ foot stalks. The 1½ inch flowers are bright red with a yellow throat. They last for one day only, yet new blossoms appear one after the other for as long as 6 weeks.

Homeria collina, var. *aurantiaca.* Similar to the type but more slender in habit, with flowers of salmon-orange flushed with scarlet.

CULTURE: The same as for gladiolus, but may be grown at a higher temperature. Use applications of manure water while buds are forming. Better purchase new corms annually.

IRIS

Included in this group are many lovely things known and loved by all gardeners. Most iris belongs in the outdoor garden; yet here and there in the genus one finds jewels for the indoor garden. Species which are too tender for outdoor culture, or plants which are suited particularly for the window garden because of size, flowering season, or fragrance. They are few in number as compared with the legion of garden species and varieties, yet all the more welcome for the fact.

Iris, *Reticulata Section*

Iris reticulata is the type plant of an important division of early-blooming irises, the reticulata group. These small irises grow from true bulbs which are characterized by a shaggy, netted coating from which the name "reticulata" originated. The diminutive plants come from Asia Minor, mostly. All are early-flowering; for the most part they are fragrant and lend themselves gracefully to indoor culture, where they may be forced into bloom a week or two before the natural flowering season.

DESCRIPTION: *Iris reticulata.* Varies from 5-10 inches in height. Out of doors it blooms early in March, often appearing before the crocuses. The flowers are violet-blue with gold centers. Leaves are narrow, four-sided, and tipped with a curious hard point. Sun shining on the flowers releases a strong, very agreeable scent of violets.

Iris reticulata danfordiae. This is the smallest of the reticulatas, flowering in February or earlier. It is a tiny, yellow-flowered plant whose standards are bristles only.

Iris reticulata histrio. The flowers, which appear in midwinter, nestle down in the center of 12 inch leaves. They are blue-purple in color, with centers of blue-streaked cream.

Iris reticulata krelagei. A very early-flowering reticulata, somewhat variable in color, although red is present usually in the blue or violet. Blossoms are shorter and broader than is common in the type, and not as fragrant.

Iris reticulata vartani. January often finds this immigrant from Palestine in bloom. The flowers are gray-blue, veined white, and touched with gold.

Iris reticulata, var. Cantab. This variety is similar to the type, but flowers are blue, orange, and white. Blooms several weeks later than *I. reticulata.* Height, 3-4 inches.

Iris reticulata, var. King Caesar. Flowers are similar to the type. This reticulata is particularly hardy and disease-resistant.

CULTURE: Bulbs of all the reticulatas described may be handled in the same manner. Use regular irid potting mixture; plant the bulbs 1 inch deep and 4 inches apart each way. Planting should be made in early fall. Bulbs of hardy plants require a strong root structure before top-growth is allowed to develop. This may be accomplished by burying pots containing the iris bulbs in cold frames or trenches out of doors, covering them with 1 foot of ashes or sand. After the bulbs have been in storage for 6-8 weeks, examine the pots. If roots project through the vent they are ready to be taken

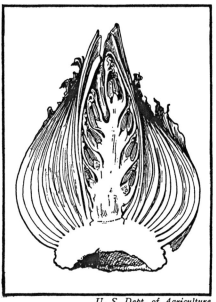

U. S. Dept. of Agriculture
FIG. 3

into the house. If no roots show, let the containers remain covered for a week or two longer. Also, bulbs may be stored in a cool cellar (45-50 degrees), by placing the pots on a pile of earth or slightly dampened sawdust. Cover with 6 inches of peat moss.

When sufficient roots have formed, bring the pot, or pots, into a cool room for growing. No sun at first, and not too much light. Wait until top-growth is well developed before maximum light is supplied. Water moderately, increasing moisture when buds begin to form. After flowering, continue to grow until leaves start to turn yellow; then remove bulbs from containers, clean and dry them, and store in a cool, dry place (in a bag containing peat moss) until fall-planting time.

As opposed to corms, most true bulbs, when properly ripened, may be used over and over again. Yet remember this. Bulb foliage must be allowed to grow until it begins to die off of its own accord. Otherwise the bulb will not have an opportunity to manufacture the following year's foliage and flowers; and blind plants will be the result.

Figure 3 shows the cross section of a narcissus bulb made in late fall. You will notice that the embryo flower spike is well developed already, months in advance of the blooming season.

HERMODACTYLUS

Related to the reticulata irises is a strange little cousin which grows from a tuber instead of a bulb. It is called the widow iris, *Hermodactylus tuberosus*. Out of the house the plant usually flowers from the middle to the last of March. In the window garden, bloom may be expected earlier, in February.

The widow iris, called also snakeshead iris, is delicately scented. The standards are lustrous apple-green in color, and the falls are of rich purple. It is a striking combination.

CULTURE: Plant the largest tubers you can buy just under

the surface of the soil in regular irid potting mixture, to which add a little more bone meal. Plant in late fall and set the pot away in a cool dark place for one month. Then bring into a location which remains cool, yet where the sun may shine on the plants for several hours daily. The principal thing to remember in flowering hermodactylus indoors is to start it and grow it in a cool temperature always. It will not force rapidly. After flowering, when the leaves have started to turn, give the tubers a thorough drying during the summer. Replant in the fall.

Iris, *Xiphium Section*

In this group of bulbous irises there are hybrid races known as Dutch, Spanish, and English iris; all developed in Holland from species indigenous to the Mediterranean region.

They are excellent plants, used in gardens extensively, as well as being in great demand for winter cut flowers at florists.

Although the natural blooming period is late spring, bulbs of several varieties are pre-cooled and treated for forcing into flower any time after the middle of December. Bulbs so treated make good house plants, yet it is a waste of time and effort to attempt the forcing of untreated bulbs. Varieties suitable for house culture are indicated as such in most dealers' catalogues.

DESCRIPTION: *Iris,* Wedgewood. This is the Xiphium most generally used for forcing. The general effect of the flowers is deep, rich blue, although there is a distinctive yellow blotch at the top of each fall.

Iris, David Bless. Similar to Wedgewood, but the flowers are of brighter blue and average lighter in color.

Iris, Imperator. Very much like the two varieties above; the flowers, however, are larger than either.

Iris, Yellow Queen. A Dutch iris of fine uniform yellow. Large flowers on tall stems.

Iris, *Crested (Evansia) Section*

This group of irises represents a small yet very distinctive class with flowers in which the beard is replaced by a crest. Better known members of this class include *Iris cristata,* and its smaller form, *Iris lacustris* from the Great Lakes region. *Iris tectorum,* the roof iris, is found in this classification, too, as well as a number of irises from foreign lands which are lovely, yet too tender for out-of-doors cultivation in most parts of the United States; still they make excellent plants for growing in the conservatory or window garden.

Two of the tender Evansias are particularly appealing. The following description of them is in the words of the late W. R. Dykes who no longer is here to applaud the iris clan, yet whose knowledge and love of the plants will leave its mark for many generations to come.

DESCRIPTION: *Iris watti.* ". . . the rhizome is very slender and sends out wide-running, stoloniferous growths. The stem, which is distinctly flattened, may be as much as three feet high, above half an inch broad, and bears a leaf on alternate sides at each node. The internodes become eventually about three inches long. Leaves may be as much as three inches broad at their middle, and have a polished upper sur-

face. All six segments of the flower are extended horizon-
tally and droop slightly at their extremities. Standards are of
plain mauve-white color, with a blunt, widely emarginate
end. The falls have a short, broad, triangular haft and an oblong blade with a finely-serrate edge, which becomes waved
at the extremity. Along the center of the haft and on to the
blade runs a raised orange-yellow ridge, which becomes very
prominent on the blade where it is surrounded by a small
patch of orange-yellow. It is flanked on each side along the
haft by two or three rows of orange blotches. The color of
the falls is a pale mauve-white, with mottlings of deeper
mauve. The filaments are of pale mauve-white, the anthers
white, and the pollen cream."

Iris japonica. "To this class (Evansia) belongs *japonica*,
or *fimbriata*, with innumerable pale mauve flowers with
yellow crests. It will not flower out of doors, and indoors its
roots should not be allowed too much room."

Iris tectorum, and its white variety may be flowered inside, too.

Iris milesi comes from the Himalayas. It has broad, bright
green leaves 2 feet or more in length. Tall, branched stalks
carry rather small lilac-red flowers, blotched with a deeper
color, and the crests are yellow. This is too large a plant
for the average window garden, but does well in the greenhouse.

Iris, Nada, was exhibited at the 1940 Boston Flower Show
as a house plant. It is a hybrid of *Iris japonica* x *Iris milesi,*
and is most attractive. The plant is about 24 inches in height.
Flowers are 2 inches across, pale lilac, with orange crests and

HYBRID CRESTED IRIS, NADA. Page 98

Antholyza paniculata. Page 81

HYBRID IXIA. Page 99

blotches. Each blossom lasts for one day. The flower stalks are thin, wiry, and much-branched; each branch carrying one or two terminal buds and flowers. There are from 14-20 flowers on each stalk. Fan-like leaf clusters are carried on sturdy, sheathed leafstalks which are from 4-10 inches in length. Individual leaves are sword-shaped and bright green.

CULTURE: The irises described above are relatively easy to flower in the house. Use small containers and regular irid potting mixture. Root systems are an important factor. A two-weeks' period in a dark cool place immediately after planting is advisable. When the leaves begin to turn, give rhizomes a good baking in the sun before resting the plants. It is probable that *Iris watti* and *japonica* will not flower until the second year after planting.

IXIA

South African bulbous herbs growing from small corms. Leaves are grass-like, generally 2-ranked. The flower stalks vary in height with the species or variety, but all are thin and wiry. Flowers are pendulous, bell-shaped, and show colors and markings from crimson and scarlet to shades of yellow and orange. In several species dark splotches occur at the base of the petals. An unusual species is *Ixia viridiflora* with metallic green flowers of surprising beauty. Late spring-blooming.

DESCRIPTION: *Ixia azurea.* Clear blue flowers, with centers of purple. Height, 12 inches.

Ixia incarnata. Intensely fragrant, tubular, pale blue flowers. Height, 2 feet. Sometimes dwarfed as a potted plant.

Ixia viridiflora. Green flowers with blue-black centers. Height, 15 inches.

Ixia, Bloem Erf. A hybrid which grows to 5 feet. Flowers are borne in branched racemes, and are colored in soft tones of pink and blue, often with an opalescent sheen.

Available also are numerous named hybrid ixias developed in Holland. The group offers a veritable rainbow of colors. All are tall-growing and very floriferous. Some of the best include: Bridesmaid, white flowers with crimson centers; Conqueror, orange-red, deep yellow inside; Englishton, old rose; Grand Duc, creamy-white, streaked and spotted with carmine; Hogarth, creamy-yellow, with purple eye; Hubert, coppery-red, shaded violet; Invincible, also called Monarch, red-purple; Marvellous, yellow and orange, with violet eye; Rossini, deep pink; Vulcan, scarlet; Wonder, double pink flowers.

CULTURE: Ixia should be forced in the manner described for hardy bulbs. 4-6 corms should be planted in 5 inch pots in the fall, using regular irid potting mixture. Keep the pots out of doors until the weather turns cool, but do not allow frost to touch them. Then bring inside to a location where temperature averages 55 degrees. Ixia, like freesia, requires slow forcing always; otherwise flowering is most unsatisfactory. After blooming, gradually withhold water and give the corms a good baking in the sun, either indoors or out; then rest the corms for several months.

LAPEYROUSIA

South African irids growing from corms. Although these plants have been in cultivation for a long time, they seldom are seen in window gardens. Plants are low-growing, with starry flowers in brilliant colors. The 6 petal segments are almost equal in size. In addition to making splendid pot plants, lapeyrousia may be grown out of doors if treated like gladiolus; welcome in the rock garden. Basal, 2-ranked leaves—from 1-8 according to species—grow from the corms; and the plants are summer-flowering.

Several species, in particular *L. cruenta* and *L. juncea,* are listed in many catalogues under anomatheca. Lapeyrousia also may be spelled lapeirousia.

DESCRIPTION: *Lapeyrousia corymbosa.* Produces but 1 narrow leaf, ribbed, and about 6 inches long. The bright or pale violet flowers are carried in a dense panicle; and other scattered flowers occur at tips of numerous small branches. Flower stalks are short and flattened; spathe-valves are green with brown tips.

Lapeyrousia fissifolia. The single, ribbed leaf is 1-4 inches in length. Violet or whitish flowers are carried on a 3 inch spike. The flower tubes are longer than in above species.

Lapeyrousia juncea. The 4-6 strap-shaped leaves are 6 inches long and about ¾ of an inch broad. Flowers are arranged in a loose spike; they are rose-pink in color and the lower segments are spotted at the throat.

Numerous other species are in cultivation.

CULTURE: Lapeyrousia grows readily from seed, often flowering within a year. Seed mixtures of such species as *L. aculeata, L. anceps, L. corymbosa, L. cruenta, L. divaricata, L. fissifolia,* and *L. jacquini* are on the market. Sow in flats, pots, or bulb pans.

Also corms may be planted in late winter or early spring and handled like gladiolus. Use regular irid potting mixture.

LIBERTIA

Seldom-grown plants of the iris family from Asia, Australia, and South America. The 12-18 inch leaves are 2-ranked, and flower stalks grow to 3 feet. Flowers occur in numerous umbels. The plants grow from short, creeping rootstocks, division of which provides the usual method of propagation.

DESCRIPTION: *Libertia formosa.* A free-blooming form, native to Chile. Individual flowers are about ⅜ of an inch long, white outside, and greenish-brown within. Leaves are numerous.

Libertia grandiflora. Very similar to *L. formosa* but larger in all its parts.

CULTURE: Plant rootstocks, one to a pot, in regular irid potting mixture. Handle like *Iris watti* and *japonica.* Hardy in the extreme south only.

MELASPHAERULA

A South African genus containing but one species; closely connected with ixia. Flowers are borne in spikes, one to a spathe. The plant differs from ixia in having arched, one-sided stamens.

DESCRIPTION: *Melasphaerula graminea.* Grows from a small rounded corm about ½ inch in diameter. The linear leaves usually are 6 in number, in a 2-ranked basal rosette. Length, 6-12 inches. Flowers are borne in few-flowered spikes. They are yellowish-green, veined in purple-black. Each flower is ½-¾ inch across. Early spring-blooming.

CULTURE: The same as for ixia, which see.

MOREA

(*Moraea*)

Iris-like plants from South Africa, Tropical Africa, Australia, Tasmania, and Lord Howe Island. True iris, strangely enough, does not occur south of the equator, in the wild. Below this belt morea takes its place. This irid grows from corms or rhizomes, and is not as hardy as iris. While the group has much in common with iris, there are certain definite botanical differences. For instance, the stigmas of morea flowers are not always petal-shaped as they are in iris, and flower scapes produce several blossoms instead of one. Too, flowers in the genus last for just one day, or less, while those of iris are quite long-lived.

Recently, morea species with evergreen foliage and rhizomes have been placed in another genus, *Dietes;* but to prevent confusion in catalogue listings the new classification will be ignored in this book and all described plants entered under morea.

For years I have been writing about the splendid possibilities of the genus for window gardens, and it is with great

satisfaction that I see so many of the plants listed today in
dealers' catalogues. The fact that numerous species and hybrids are offered for sale is proof that more and more gardeners are appreciating and calling for these plants.

Flowers in many colors, and plants in many sizes are available. Certain species are less than 1 foot in height; others
reach to 6 feet and over. The larger moreas, while lovely,
are subjects for the greenhouse rather than the window garden; although that is a matter for individual choice. As
has been noted, the flowers are short-lived; yet many are
borne in succession, so the total blooming period is most satisfactory.

DESCRIPTION: *Morea catenulata.* Grows from a rhizome.
The flowers are waxy-white. Sometimes two rows of curious
little warts extend from the outer corolla segments. A low-
growing, evergreen type which flowers sporadically the year
around.

Morea glaucopis. Grows from a corm. The little peacock
iris has pure white flowers with iridescent blue spots at the
base of each outer segment. Height, 12 inches.

Morea iridioides johnsoni. Grows from a rhizome. Straight
narrow leaves which form large clumps on established
plants. Blooms several times during the summer; in fact,
this species has definite ever-blooming qualities. Flowers are
white, blotched with orange, and the style branches are
lavender. Height, 18-24 inches.

Morea isopetala. Grows from a corm. Flowers may be enjoyed throughout the year by making successive plantings.
The blossoms are lavender in color, and are carried on slender wiry branches. Height 6-8 inches.

Morea polystachya. Grows from a corm. A slender plant, 18-24 inches high, with flowers of bright mauve, penciled in violet, with a yellow spot at base of outer segments. Blooms for 3-4 months either in summer or winter according to forcing schedule.

Morea ramosa. Grows from a corm. The flowers are large, bright yellow with blue-green markings, and carried on 3-4 foot, well-branched flower stalks.

Morea tricuspis lutea. Grows from a corm. Yellow flowers, about 1½ inches across. Flower stalks are 26-30 inches in height. Blooming season, May.

Morea villosa. Grows from a corm. Similar to *M. glaucopis,* except flowers are blue instead of white.

Morea, Oakhurst. Grows from a rhizome. This fine hybrid is a cross of *M. catenulata* x *M. bicolor.* It was introduced by J. N. Giridlian in 1937. Of it the introducer says: "They make large clumps which are highly ornamental. The flowers are creamy-white, well rounded in shape, 2 inches across on 4 foot stems. Although their main blooming season is during the summer, flowers may be found on the established plants during every day of the year."

Morea robinsoniana. A 6 foot plant from Lord Howe Island in the South Seas. It is romantically interesting, for it is used by the Islanders as a wedding decoration. Flowers of pure white, with yellow and violet markings at the base of outer segments. A magnificent plant, but requires ample space for growing.

CULTURE: Moreas growing from rhizomes and those growing from corms require slightly different forcing treatment. Corms should be grown in cool locations, like ixia, with little water until growth is well started. After flowering, when leaves have ripened, the corms need a long rest and a good curing in the sun. Rhizomatous moreas require more water and do not need the long, dry resting period. Plant both corms and rhizomes in rich sandy soil free from animal manure and decayed vegetable matter. Bone meal is a good fertilizer and must be incorporated into the potting mixture very thoroughly. While plants are forming buds and blooming, they never must be allowed to become dry.

Morea may be grown from seed quite easily. If interest in the genus results in a desire to make a comprehensive collection of plants, seeds of many species are available.

NEMASTYLIS

A genus of tender North American bulbous plants containing few species. Flowers in this genus are blue, 6-lobed, fugacious, and about 1 inch in width. Leaves are few, mostly basal, and linear. The flowers are subtended by spathes, and inner segments are a little smaller than the outer segments.

DESCRIPTION: *Nemastylis coelistina.* 1-2 leaves about 1 foot long, basal; and the flower stalks carry 3-4 smaller leaves. The flowers are sky-blue. This plant is native from South Carolina to Florida and westward.

Nemastylis acuta. Southwestern United States is the habitat. The lower leaves are 6-12 inches in length, and 2-3 in number. Flowers are similar to above species and bright blue.

CULTURE: The same as for ixia, which see.

RIGIDELLA

In this genus are to be found 3 species of bulbous Mexican plants related to tigridia. They differ from the tiger flower by having small, ovoid, and erect inner flower segments, while those of tigridia are fiddle-shaped, large, and spreading. The leaves are broad, with channeled leafstalks. The flowers last for one day only, and are bright red in color.

DESCRIPTION: *Rigidella immaculata.* Flowers of this species are bright crimson, borne on stems 2-3 feet in height. The leaves are short, 1½-2 inches in length.

CULTURE: The same as for ixia, which see.

ROMULEA

A South African irid growing from a corm. Rare in cultivation and seldom grown in the window garden; although several species, and mixed seeds, are on the market. The colorful flowers resemble short-tubed gloxinias in appearance, and appear from 2-valved bracts. The leaves are linear.

DESCRIPTION: *Romulea rosea.* Flowers with yellow throat, bordered in red-lilac. The leaves are 1 foot in length and ¼-1 inch wide, ribbed. Flower stalk is about 3 inches long, bearing several short flower stems.

Romulea sabulosa. Flowers are rosy-red with a dark brown blotch at the base of each segment; bell-shaped, and up to 2 inches in length. The stiff, erect leaves are round and very thin. This species requires all the sun it can get.

CULTURE: Use regular irid potting mixture. Give the corms two weeks in a dark location after potting, then bring into the sun and warmth for growing on. After the leaves have turned, withhold water entirely and rest in a sunny place for several months. While plants are growing, keep the potting mixture damp always, but do not flood.

SCHIZOSTYLIS

The Kaffir lily (from South Africa) is better known, probably, than many of the irids described in this chapter; yet it is rare enough in window gardens to warrant inclusion here. The type flowers too late in the year to be practical in northern gardens; a variety, Mrs. Hegarty, however, may be grown outside as a summer bulbous plant; for its blossoms appear two months earlier. Both plants are useful and beautiful house specimens of easy culture.

DESCRIPTION: *Schizostylis coccinea.* Grows from a rhizome. The leaves are few, grass-like, about 18 inches long, and 2-ranked. 6-8 tubular flowers of deep crimson appear in late autumn or early winter on 1-2 foot stalks.

Schizostylis coccinea, var. Mrs. Hegarty. Possibly a distinct species instead of a variety. Grows from a rhizome. Similar to above but the flowers are soft pink and larger, although the plant is smaller. Blooming season is in late summer or early fall.

CULTURE: Plant rhizomes in regular irid potting mixture in the spring. Water regularly and often. After flowering, dry off the plants and store until March, but supply enough water from time to time to keep the root-stocks from shriveling.

SPARAXIS

Brilliant bulbous plants of the iris family, from South Africa. Flowers are starry and reminiscent of ixia, with 6 wide open segments larger than those comprising ixia blossoms. Sparaxis plants, however, are smaller than most ixias,

SPARAXIS

averaging 12-18 inches in height. Flower colors are white, yellow, orange, red, crimson, purple, and brown; and variant color combinations mark the hybrid forms, which are numerous. Sparaxis species hybridize readily with each other; also with plants in the genus, *Streptanthera*. Hybrids in the latter class are called sparanthera and are characterized by the unusual bronze and coppery shadings, and brilliant blending of colors.

The plants grow from corms, and have 2-ranked, fan-like clusters of leaves. Flowers are carried on spikes, either simple or branched, with but few flowers to a spike.

Corms of two or three species are available, and seeds of hybrids in greater variety. While seedlings will not flower as quickly as plants grown from corms, they are not difficult to bring into flower the second year after planting.

DESCRIPTION: *Sparaxis grandiflora.* A small species growing to 1 foot. The flowers are about 1 inch long, segments ½ inch wide, and the color is either yellow or purple. Several named forms have fine flowers in white, dark purple, or yellow. Leaves are narrow.

Sparaxis tricolor. Larger than above species, growing to 18 inches. Flowers usually in three different colors, but flower-throat is always yellow with a blotch at the base of each segment.

Both species flower in early spring.

CULTURE: The same as for ixia, which see.

STREPTANTHERA

South African irids, low-growing, with brilliant, 6-segmented flowers interestingly marked. Flowers are quite like those of sparaxis and ixia, and plants of these genera hybridize readily. I know of but one species available here at present.

DESCRIPTION: *Streptanthera cuprea.* Grows from a corm. The leaves are short and arranged in a fan-like cluster. Flowers are coppery-yellow, with yellow-spotted, purple throats. There are 2-4, 1 inch blossoms on each stalk. Early spring-blooming.

CULTURE: In the fall, plant in regular irid potting mixture. Bury the corms about 1 inch deep, 8 of them to a 6 inch pot. Keep the pots in a cold frame or covered in the cellar for 4-6

weeks until heavy rooting is established. Then bring inside
and grow in a cool location in the sun. After top-growth
is developed, water frequently and use manure water
monthly. *S. cuprea* should be handled like freesia.

TRITONIA

These are the irids more commonly called montbretia.
They are used extensively as garden plants, and they are excellent for forcing as well.

Tritonias grow from corms and produce fan-like rosettes
of sword-shaped leaves with one or more flower stalks;
sometimes branched, sometimes not. Flowers resemble
those of small gladioli from a distance, particularly in the
manner of growing, but are flatter. The flower-tube is cylindrical below, and funnel-shaped above. There are 6 segments, equal in some varieties, unequal in others.

One species is specifically recommended for house culture, although all the tritonias, or montbretias, may be used
with assured satisfaction.

DESCRIPTION: *Tritonia hyalina.* Grows from a corm. Flowers are salmon-pink to flame-salmon, with a hyaline or trans-
lucent area at the base of each segment. Segments are ¾-1
inch long. Purple anthers add an interesting note to the
color scheme. The 4-6 leaves are rather short, 4-8 inches,
and the flower stalks grow 12-18 inches in height bearing
5-10 flowers. Summer to autumn-flowering.

CULTURE: Plant the corms in a potting mixture consisting
of equal parts of loam, sand, and peat moss with the addition

of a handful of bone meal. Keep in a cool dark place until roots have formed. Then provide full sun and frequent watering. New corms, if they are to be planted the following season, should receive a long and thorough sun-ripening.

This chapter completes the plants in the iris family; rather, it lists most available Iridaceae for house plant purposes. The family is extensive, and undoubtedly from time to time, other irids will be placed in cultivation and offered on the market.

V

LILY FAMILY

Chapter 5

LILY FAMILY

ONE OF the best terse descriptions of the lily family which I have read is that given by Norman Taylor in the Garden Dictionary.* It is repeated herewith, for it would be difficult to improve upon.

"The lily family is of more garden importance than even its 200 genera and over 2000 species might suggest. It is sometimes called the aloe, hyacinth, or tulip family, and it has been split by botanists into four families.

1. Lily family proper (Liliaceae)
2. Lily-of-the-valley family (Convallariaceae)
3. Bunchflower family (Melanthaceae)
4. Smilax family (Smilaceae)

"As here considered, all these are grouped in one big family, the Liliaceae. They are often bulbous herbs, but some are vines (Smilax), and woody or even tree-like plants occur in *Nolina, Yucca, Samuela, Hespero-yucca, Phormium, Cordyline, Dasylirion, Dracaena,* and *Aloe,* most of which come from warm regions. Garden vegetables are found in

* *The Garden Dictionary,* by permission Houghton Mifflin, publishers.

115

Asparagus and *Allium*. But the family is noteworthy for the showy bloom of most of its numerous garden genera, especially *Lilium, Brodiaea, Bulbocodium, Calochortus, Chionodoxa, Colchicum, Convallaria, Eremurus, Erythronium, Fritillaria, Hemerocallis, Hosta, Hyacinthus, Kniphofia, Muscari, Ornithogalum, Scilla, Tulipa, Trillium, Urginea,* and *Zygadenus.*

"Some genera are chiefly greenhouse plants, notably *Agapanthus, Anthericum, Aspidistra, Chlorophytum, Eucomis, Gasteria, Gloriosa, Haworthia, Lapageria, Reineckia, Rohdea, Ruscus, Sansevieria,* and *Schizobasopsis.*

"There are, in addition, a few genera which contain native American plants, often in the woods in the East, and on prairies or the Pacific Coast in the West. They are suited to the wild garden, bog, or to other special sites . . . many have attractive flowers and are well worth the gardener's attention, but they are not so widely grown as better-known genera.

"The only other plants of horticultural interest are found in: *Asphodeline, Asphodelus, Galtonia, Lachenalia, Liriope, Ophiopogon, Paradisea, Puschkinia, Tricyrtis,* and *Veratrum.*

"The Liliaceae has alternate leaves, nearly always stalkless, generally without marginal teeth. In nearly all the herbs the stem arises from a bulb, very prominent in the onion and tulip, less so in some other genera, and replaced by a root-stock in many genera.

"Flowers nearly always very showy, typically of 6 segments, indistinguishable as to calyx or corolla, or in some genera tubular. While solitary flowers are not uncommon (tulip, *Erythronium,* etc.) generally the flowers are in clusters, the raceme being the most common form of inflorescence. But umbels and umbel-like clusters occur in *Smilax, Allium,* and several other genera. The ovary is superior in all but two genera (*Liriope* and *Ophiopogon*), and this is the chief difference between this family and the Amaryllidaceae, which has an inferior ovary. Stamens mostly 6, rarely 3. Fruit a berry or a capsule."

The name "Lily" is somewhat confusing at times, for it is used loosely in many common names for plants with tubular or chalice-shaped flowers—plants which do not belong to the lily family. Common examples of this nomenclature include:

Waterlily (*Nymphaea*)	Fairy lily (*Zephyranthes*)
Blackberry lily (*Belamcanda*)	Guernsey lily (*Nerine*)
	Jacobean lily (*Sprekelia*)
Belladonna lily (*Amaryllis*)	Kaffir lily (*Schizostylis*)
Mystery lily (*Lycoris*)	Scarborough lily (*Vallota*)
Spider lily (*Hymenocallis*)	Rain lily (*Cooperia*)
Calla lily (*Zantedeschia*)	Lily-of-the-field (*Sternbergia*)
Amazon lily (*Eucharis*)	

In addition to the above there are many plants in whose common names "Lily" appears that are members of the lily family, but not of the genus *Lilium.* It is distracting to pursue the subject any further, so it will be dropped right here.

Good house plant types are to be found in the lily family, both in familiar and little-known genera. Not as many of the rarer plants are in cultivation as an enthusiast might wish; yet there are a few, and they are all worth while.

In addition to plants described in this chapter, most of which are notable for lovely flowers, there are some fine succulents in the genera *Aloe, Gasteria,* and *Haworthia.* As specimens of these succulents appear regularly in many

2 parts loam
2 parts sand
1 part leaf mold
½ part old cow manure
½ part bone meal

LILY POTTING MIXTURE

window gardens, no further mention will be made of them here. However, a full description of these plants and numerous other cacti and succulents may be found in "Grow Them Indoors."

A general potting mixture for most plants in the lily family is shown on the chart.

ALBUCA

Tender bulbous plants of the lily family from the Cape of Good Hope region, related to ornithogalum. Rare and very seldom grown, but available.

DESCRIPTION: *Albuca aurea.* Grows from a bulb. Large sprays of numerous pale yellow, upright flowers are carried on medium-sized stalks. The flower bracts are yellow.

Albuca major. This species produces 6-15 greenish-yellow, nodding flowers with red bracts.

CULTURE: The same as for ornithogalum.

ANDROSTEPHIUM

A small genus indigenous to S. W. United States, with funnel-shaped flowers and basal, linear leaves which usually are grass-like. The flowering season is in early spring.

DESCRIPTION: *Androstephium violaceum* (syn. *coeruleum*). Grows from a bulb. A slender plant growing 6-10 inches high. The flowers are about 1 inch long, 3-6 in a loose umbel, and a lovely blue in color. The leaves are very numerous.

CULTURE: Regular lily potting mixture, with the addition of more sand. Pot in the fall and handle like other hardy bulbs. Rest and ripen the bulbs after flowering.

BESSERA

Bessera elegans is the name under which you will find this attractive little Mexican bulbous plant listed. Its true botanical name is *Milla biflora*. This name, too, is somewhat confusing, for all plants—except this one—formerly assigned to the genus *Milla,* are now included under *Brodiaea*. However, leaving aside any difficulties in nomenclature, the little plant provides a lovely and tractable subject for indoor culture under any of its several names. Blooms in winter or early spring indoors depending upon planting schedule.

MILLA BIFLORA

DESCRIPTION: *Milla biflora*. Grows from a bulb. Leaves are basal and grass-like. The fragrant white flowers, over 2 inches wide, are carried in clusters of 3-5 atop naked flower stalks 12-24 inches in height.

CULTURE: Regular lily potting mixture. Use 4 bulbs to a 6 inch pot and figure on about 3 months from planting to blooming. For further growing instructions, follow those for forcing gladiolus indoors.

BLANDFORDIA

Tender bulbous plants from Tasmania and Australia related to funkia and kniphofia. From numerous ribbon-like,

2-ranked leaves, flower stalks arise to 18-24 inches bearing 4-12 large, nodding flowers in short racemes. Flowers open in late winter or early spring.

DESCRIPTION: *Blandfordia flammea.* Grows from a tuberous root. The leaves are 12-18 inches long, 2-2½ inches wide. The bell-shaped flowers are usually orange-red to crimson, with yellow tips; yet they may be all red or entirely yellow. Individual flowers are 1½-3 inches long.

CULTURE: The potting soil should consist mostly of peat (not peat moss) together with some sand and charcoal. A moist atmosphere and lots of air are required, as well as biweekly applications of manure water during the growing season. Plant roots in late summer and force gently until top-growth appears. Then water regularly and provide ample light, without sun, until buds are formed. Use small containers and keep the plants partially rootbound for best results.

BRODIAEA

A group of about 30 species of California herbs (Liliaceae) growing from corms. The genus now includes plants formerly separated under the genera *Brevoortia, Calliprora, Hesperoscordum, Hookera, Milla,* and *Triteleia.* Certain of the species make satisfactory plants for the outdoor garden; nearly all are good pot plants for indoor use.

Mostly, brodiaea corms produce grassy, basal leaves and slender, naked flower stalks bearing umbels of waxy flowers which are beautiful and long-lasting. Blooming schedules may be arranged, for forced corms, from February until late in the summer. The following list of brodiaeas is taken from the catalogue of a well-known western grower. Corms are available from September to December.

DESCRIPTION: *Brodiaea californica.* This is one of the two plants commonly called Harvest Brodiaea. It is the largest and tallest of all brodiaeas. It grows from 1-2 feet high with stout stems crowned with an umbel of 8-12 flowers. Very late and lasting. Two color forms: deep blue, tinted lilac-rose, or soft lilac-pink.

Brodiaea candida. Rather like *B. laxa,* with very fine, delicate lilac flowers; each pedicel bent to make the flowers face one way.

Brodiaea capitata. Called the California Hyacinth. It has slender stems 6-12 inches high, capped with a close cluster of violet-blue flowers.

Brodiaea coccinea. The Floral Firecracker. This has tubular red flowers tipped with yellow. Grows to 18 inches in height.

Brodiaea crocea. Grows 6-9 inches high and has clear yellow flowers.

Brodiaea douglassi. This species has a slender stem and porcelain-blue flowers.

Brodiaea eastwoodi. Umbels like *B. laxa* but with flowers of pure white. Needs lots of water.

Brodiaea grandiflora. The other Harvest Brodiaea. Large, glossy purple flowers of long life.

Brodiaea hendersoni. Stems 8-12 inches high. Flowers are yellow, banded with purple.

Brodiaea ixioides splendens. Numerous fine flowers of clear yellow.

Brodiaea lactea. Cupped flowers of milky-white, with green midveins.

Brodiaea laxa. 1-2 feet in height with numerous flowers of clear blue.

Brodiaea purdyi. Grows to about 6 inches. Broad-spreading flowers of reddish-lilac. Tips of segments are recurved in an interesting manner.

Brodiaea stellaris. Low-growing. Starry blue flowers with contrasting white centers.

Brodiaea volubilis. A species which climbs to four feet if supported. The flowers are pink.

CULTURE: Brodiaea corms should be handled like hardy bulbs. Pot in the fall and allow them to form heavy root systems in a cool dark place before top-growth is encouraged. Use regular lily potting mixture, and water frequently after growth begins to develop, but be sure there is ample drainage in the container. Plant new corms each year for best results.

CALOCHORTUS

A large genus of western North American bulbous herbs belonging to the lily family. About 40 species are recognized all of which grow from corms. Flower stalks are erect and leaves are grass-like mostly, although some are quite fleshy. Calochorti vary considerably in form and blooming season. As a matter of convenience the different types have been divided tentatively into sections. Calochortus is grown in eastern gardens with varying degrees of success, but all of the species make good subjects for window gardens. Normal flowering time is March to June; earlier indoors.

Calochortus, *Section A*

Globe Tulips

Globe tulips, or fairy lanterns, have globular flowers with a satiny sheen. The plants are tall, slender, and more leafy

CALOCHORTUS

than species in the other sections; with a long leaf at the base of the flower stalk and smaller leaves above.

DESCRIPTION: *Calochortus albus.* Branched, with numerous flowers of pure white. Grows 8-10 inches high.

Calochortus amabilis. Flowers of clean rich yellow marked externally with brown patches. Grows 10-15 inches high.

Calochortus amoenus. Similar to *C. albus,* but flowers are rose-pink. Grows 8 inches high.

Calochortus amoenus major. A larger variety of above, growing 20-24 inches in height.

Calochortus, *Section B*

Star Tulips

This section contains calochorti with slender stalks and narrow leaves that usually rest upon the ground. Flowers are upturned, delicate, and lined with fine hairs, which has given the group its other common name—cat's ears. Many pastel shades are typical of star tulip flowers. Flowering season is March to May outside, later in eastern gardens, and earlier in the house.

DESCRIPTION: *Calochortus benthami.* Bright yellow flowers, sometimes marked with black at base of segments. Grows 4-8 inches high.

Calochortus maweanus major. A fine species with white flowers and lavender hairs. Larger than above.

Calochortus lilacinus. Fragrant flowers of clear lilac. Grows to 8 inches.

Calochortus, *Section C*

Mariposa Tulips

The mariposa or butterfly tulips represent the prize plants in the genus. They are tall-growing with but few small leaves scattered along the flower stalks. The flowers are exquisite. They are 3-4 inches across, in white and various colors, eyed or feathered in brilliant contrasting shades, with areas of soft colorful hairs.

DESCRIPTION: *Calochortus howelli.* Flowers white and

slightly reflexed. Greenish hairs at the base of petals. Grows 10-12 inches high.

Calochortus kennedyi. Inside of flowers is blazing vermilion; exteriors, yellow.

Calochortus leichtlini. Flowers are of unusual cloudy-white with patches of deep purple. The petal bases are tinted with greenish-lilac, sometimes greenish-yellow. Grows 8-10 inches in height.

Calochortus superbus. Tall-growing and branched. Flowers are white inside, lavender outside. A penciled, maroon eye nestles at the petal bases.

Calochortus venustus citrinus. Rich yellow flowers, eyed with black.

Calochortus venustus oculatus. Similar to *C. citrinus,* but the huge flowers are white, or creamy-white, tinted with purple. The eyes are deep black and lustrous in some plants, variously colored in others.

Calochortus vesta. A sun-loving species. Flowers are 3-5 inches across; white, flushed with lilac. They are red at the center and purple on outside of petals. A good plant in every respect. If you grow no other calochortus, try this one.

Calochortus, *Section C1*

Nitidus-lyalli Group

This is a sub-section of mariposa tulips from a colder region than plants in Section C. Flowers are similar in structure, but there is only one lance-shaped, basal leaf.

DESCRIPTION: *Calochortus apiculatus.* The flowers are soft yellow and hairy.

Calochortus eurycarpus. Bears umbels of white, lavender-marked, flowers blotched with purple.

Calochortus greeni. Large, cup-like flowers of lilac with yellow petal bases.

Calochortus nitidus. Flowers are pale lavender and unspotted.

Calochortus lyalli. Flowers are white, barred inside with purple.

There are numerous calochorti available in the first three sections other than those listed here.

CULTURE: Use a potting mixture consisting of: one part good loam; one part leaf mold; one part sharp sand; several lumps of charcoal. Be sure of ample drainage material. Corms are planted in the fall, several to a small pot. Treat as hardy bulbs, allowing for a substantial root system to form before bringing plants into the light. After flowering, dry off gradually and ripen new corms in the sun for 45-60 days. A long, dry rest is indicated in late summer and early autumn if new corms are expected to blossom. To be on the safe side, plan to purchase and plant a few new corms each fall. Aside from their marked beauty as growing plants, calochorti make splendid cut flowers.

CHLOROGALUM

In this genus are about 3 species of bulbous plants native to the west coast of the United States. They are related to camassia and zygadenus. One chlorogalum is in general cultivation. Although it is not as striking in appearance as are many other members of the lily family, it is an interesting addition to the window garden collection. From its bulb the Indians made soap many years ago; and today chlorogalum is an important bee plant.

DESCRIPTION: *Chlorogalum pomeridianum.* Grows from a large bulb. Flowers are carried in large panicles on leafy stalks growing to 3 feet in the house, up to 5 feet in the garden. Blossoms are star-like, about 1 inch across, and white with purple veining. The leaves are long and wavy-margined at the base, becoming smaller and fewer in number towards the top of the stalk.

CULTURE: The same as for ornithogalum.

ERYTHRONIUM

ERYTHRONIUM

A genus of about 12 spring-blooming, bulbous herbs of the lily family. With one exception—*Erythronium denscanis,* a European species—the rest of the genus is North American; members occurring throughout the United States, east and west. Several common names are ascribed to erythronium; such as, dogtooth violet, trout lily, and adder's tongue.

The flowers of this group are handsome, as are the basal

leaves which are 2 in number, occasionally bright clear green; but more often mottled and marbled with dark areas. All species and varieties grow from true bulbs, most of which are long, white, and bear resemblance to a dog's fang.

Certain species respond better to forcing than do others. Those listed herewith are dependable performers, and may be had in flower as early as Christmas. Other erythroniums may be forced, too; yet require special growing conditions to prevent flowers from opening before flower stalks have attained normal height; and sessile erythronium blossoms are not desirable.

DESCRIPTION: *Erythronium californicum*. Large cream-colored flowers and heavily mottled leaves. Several flowers are produced on each flower stalk.

Erythronium californicum bicolor. The outer half of the flower petals is pure white, the inner half is chrome yellow. Blossoms of this plant are deliciously scented. More than one flower to each stalk.

Erythronium hartwegi. Flowers resemble those of *E. californicum,* but contain more yellow in the perianth, and only one flower is carried to a stem.

Erythronium hendersoni. Flowers are of bright purple, with deep maroon centers. One flower to each stalk.

CULTURE: Regarding the above erythroniums, Mr. Carl Purdy of California writes me as follows:

"After rooting, taking them into a house or greenhouse at 50-55 degrees simply brings spring conditions to them sooner; just as a greatly advanced season here in the west will bring them out as much as three months ahead of normal.

Bottom heat, however, aside from being unnecessary, is disastrous to the bulbs.

"Erythroniums respond well, but as a rule I would limit them to E. californicum, E. californicum bicolor, E. hartweggi, and E. hendersoni. Erythronium grandiflorum if brought to the flowering point more slowly in a cool house would do, but tends to have short stems if pushed too rapidly.

"I have no data on erythroniums of the Revolutum group, aside from some grown during several years past for exhibit at the New York Flower Show. Under natural conditions this group matures somewhat more slowly than the other group, and if pushed too rapidly has flowers almost in the soil. Grown in electrically heated frames the first attempts brought just this result, but later attempts, where brought on at temperatures around 40-45 degrees to the point where buds showed on good stems, and then taking into temperatures of 55 degrees, produced good flowers.

"Those named above are all quite easy, and with most crude treatment we have had them in flower in the house by Christmas. E. hartweggi, potted December 15 and rooted in two weeks, was introduced into a temperature of 50-55 degrees and flowered January 19 with good stems; while in the same trial others mentioned came on 4-8 days later.

"Without having been familiar with the varied seasons here in California it is hard to realize how adaptable and responsive to seasonable conditions our plants must be in order to reach maturity and produce their seeds. I have seen cool winters which ended by February 1, with a change to warm and dry weather where practically all flowers that normally flower from March 1 to June would push forth

MOREA, OAKHURST HYBRID. Page 105

SPARAXIS. Page 109

PINEAPPLE LILY (*Eucomis punctata*). Page 130

their growth and flower within three to four weeks, the late ones often flowering with large seed production with flowers and stems just out of the ground, where in normal seasons they would reach their usual heights of 1-3 feet.

"The necessity of such responsiveness to seasons makes all of our bulbous subjects, except those from quite cool regions, good house or greenhouse subjects."

Use regular lily potting mixture, and plant bulbs in the early fall. Root and grow them in a cool place. After the leaves have matured, ripen and rest the bulbs before re-using.

EUCOMIS

A small genus of South African bulbous plants of the lily family. Two species are in cultivation. They are related to scilla and make fine house, or greenhouse, subjects.

DESCRIPTION: *Eucomis punctata*. The pineapple lily grows from a bulb. Flowers are 6-stamened, about ½ inch in length, greenish-white to purple in color, and borne in leafy-crowned racemes. The leaves are purple or brown-spotted on the under side, about 2 feet long and 3 inches wide, growing in a basal rosette. Height 1-2 feet.

Eucomis undulata. Grows from an ovate bulb. The royal crown plant has long, spreading or recurving leaves, oblong in shape. Numerous green or yellowish-green flowers are carried on scapes about 2 feet in height, surmounted by a canopy of leaves.

CULTURE: Plant in regular lily potting mixture. Root first, then bring into the house and grow in a cool location. Rest the bulbs after leaves have turned. The bulbs of eucomis are half-hardy, yet of little use in outdoor gardens north of Washington.

GLORIOSA

A genus of weak-stemmed, tuberous-rooted, climbing plants from Asia and Tropical Africa. The 2-4 inch flowers resemble speciosum lilies in shape and often in coloring. They are borne singly in upper leaf axils. Support for climbing is accomplished by extended leaf-points which become tendrils.

GLORIOSA

While gloriosa is not the most amenable of house plants, it may be flowered indoors without much trouble providing its requirements are met. In northern gardens, members of the genus are grown as summer annuals, the roots being stored over winter in sand or peat moss. Plants may grow 10 feet in height or over, or they may be kept smaller at the grower's discretion. Summer-flowering.

DESCRIPTION: *Gloriosa planti.* When grown in the shade, flowers of this species are clear yellow in color. Exposure to sun brings tints of tangerine and scarlet to the petals.

Gloriosa rothschildiana. Bears large, recurved flowers of

crimson; sometimes rose-tinted, sometimes edged with golden-yellow. The segments often are wavy, but are not
crisped. A tall-growing plant.

Gloriosa superba. A smaller plant than the above species.
The flowers open yellow, later changing to red. Segments
are crisped and twisted. This is the species most commonly
grown.

Gloriosa virescens. Scarlet flowers marked with yellow.
An excellent species, rare, yet available.

CULTURE: Plant the tuberous roots in lily potting mixture,
1 root to a pot. Plant in late January or February for summer and autumn bloom. Grow in a temperature of 55-65
degrees; no rooting period necessary. After blooming reduce
watering to allow the plant to rest. A suitable support will
be necessary for each plant.

HELONIAS

A bulbous perennial herb native to swamps and bogs of
eastern United States, from New Jersey south to the Caro-
linas. It is grown in bog gardens and moist wild plantings;
and it makes a splendid pot plant for the house as well.
There is but one species in the genus; it flowers in early
spring, April-May.

DESCRIPTION: *Helonias bullata.* Commonly called swamp
or stud pink. The leaves are several or numerous, basal, from
6-15 inches in length and ½-2 inches wide. Flowers are
white, pink, or purplish, borne in 1-3 inch racemes on 1-2
foot, hollow, bracted stalks. Each flower has 6 lobes, is about
½ inch wide, and has 6 bright blue anthers.

CULTURE: Helonias requires an acid soil. Plant in regular lily potting mixture to which has been added some peat and oak leaf humus. Handle as you would any hardy bulb. This plant needs lots of water during the active season of growth; ripen and rest after flowering.

LACHENALIA

LACHENALIA

Lachenalias, or Cape cowslips, are an important group of small South African plants growing from tunicated bulbs. Numerous species and horticultural varieties are in cultivation; and new species are being recognized constantly.

Flowers are borne in spikes on heavy, fleshy stalks: they are not unlike small hyacinths or the blossoms of some aloes, but the plants are different. Three and four colors appear in each flower of certain species; other flower spikes are clothed in more modest tones wherein green is a predominant factor. There are two types of lachenalia. One is small-flowered, the other has larger, longer, and more tubular blossoms.

Small-flowered lachenalias hybridize readily, and consid-

erable attention has been accorded this trait, with the result
that quite a few fine hybrids are on the market.

The leaves are few, usually 2, basal, and often spotted.
They are strap or lance-shaped and seldom exceed 12 inches
in length; usually they are much shorter. The plants are of
easy culture and flower freely in late winter or early spring.

DESCRIPTION: *Lachenalia aurea.* This is a variety of *L. tricolor,* with flowers of bright orange-yellow. Leaves, 2, 6-9
inches long, and about 1 inch wide at the center. The flower
stalk varies from 6-12 inches in height carrying few or numerous cylindrical flowers.

Lachenalia liliflora. A small species with pink flowers
prettily tinged with blue.

Lachenalia nelsoni. In this plant the yellow flowers are
marked with green.

Lachenalia orchioides. The flowers are red, blue, yellow,
or white; usually they are yellow, red-tipped, with green
shadings. The flower spike is small, as are the individual
flowers (about 1/3 inch long).

Lachenalia purpureo-caerulea. In this species a heavy, 6
inch flower stalk carries bell-shaped blossoms of blue-purple.

Lachenalia pustula. The 2 leaves are fleshy, $\frac{1}{2}$-1 inch wide,
and covered with papillae. Red-tinged or white flowers are
carried in a dense 2-3 inch spike.

Lachenalia, Rector of Cawston. A beautiful hybrid with
flowers of yellow, green, and scarlet.

Lachenalia rubida. The 2 lance-shaped leaves are about 6
inches long and 1 inch wide, spotted. 6-20, 1 inch flowers
are produced in each cluster. They are red outside, tipped
with green. Petal interiors are yellow.

Lachenalia tricolor. One of the best lachenalias for house culture. Similar in size to *L. aurea,* but flowers are green-tipped-yellow outside, purple-red within.

Lachenalia unicolor. The 2 leaves are covered with papillae. Small, bright red flowers occur in spikes 3-6 inches in height.

Lachenalia unifolia. The single leaf is long and slender, brown where it clasps the flower stalk. Flowers are carried in a rather loose raceme, 6-20 in number, and white, tinged with red or blue.

CULTURE: Use a potting mixture of: one part loam; one part sand; one part leaf mold; and surround the bulbs with a layer of sand. Plant in late fall, 5 bulbs to a 6 inch pot; one-half inch of soil above the points of the bulbs. Place in a dark cool room and water sparingly until top-growth is 2 inches in height. Then place in the light for flowering. Rest and ripen the bulbs after the leaves have turned yellow.

LILIUM

One of the most important genera in the lily family—the true lilies. About 100 species are known from Europe, Asia, and North America. During the past decade innumerable hybrids have been produced, the best of which comprise a select group of distinct garden importance.

Lilies are perennial herbs growing from scaly bulbs. The flowers are very beautiful and showy, either nodding, erect, or horizontal. Leaves are narrow in most species, scattered along the flower stalk or ascending it in whorls.

It may seem strange and out of place to include this popular genus in a book about lesser-known house plants; yet the lilies have been given a place here for the same reason that gladiolus was accorded mention. Because, other than the ubiquitous Easter lily and an occasional speciosum variety, but few of the genus are grown in window gardens; although many species lend themselves admirably to growing indoors and early blooming. While forced lilies are not graced with the intense fragrance which characterizes some species flowered naturally in the garden, the dereliction is considered by most window gardeners as an asset rather than a liability. Plants, too, are smaller usually when grown in pots; yet are inherently beautiful in any size as to flower form and color.

Culture is not difficult, and most lily bulbs flowered in the house may be ripened and planted in the outdoor garden for permanent occupancy, or they may be used over and over again in the window garden if handled properly. There are species, however, which are too tender for dependable tenancy in northern gardens. These plants may be enjoyed inside in latitudes where otherwise their gay trumpets or chalices would never be known, except from pale replicas reflected in garden books and magazine articles.

Certain species will be listed in this entry, including a few of the rarer lilies. All have been grown as house plants with relative ease. Lack of space prevents a listing of all available lilies, but where you have one or more pet members of the genus that you would like to flower indoors—species which are not included in this tabulation,—go right ahead and grow them, following the instructions given below. Many will prove to be just as amenable as the ones described.

DESCRIPTION: *Lilium auratum.* Large flowers of white with a crimson-dotted, yellow band down the middle of each petal. In addition to the type there are several other forms.

Lilium auratum platyphyllum (syn. *macranthum*). This variety has similar but larger flowers than the type. Also it is more robust and permanent.

Lilium auratum rubrovittatum. A sport of the type, with petal bands of crimson which are yellow at base of segment.

Lilium auratum pictum. Another variant form. The petal tips are flushed with crimson, and the flower is more heavily spotted.

Lilium auratum, var. Crimson Queen. This variety is supposed to be a hybrid of *L. auratum platyphyllum* x *L. speciosum melpomene.* The flowers are suffused with rosy-pink, spotted with deep rose, and the petal stripes are crimson-rose.

Lilium auratum virginale (syn. *wittei*). An albino form. Unspotted, but the yellow petal band is present.

Lilium candidum. The madonna or annunciation lily is a European species which has been cultivated for centuries; and it is still one of the most popular lilies to be found in any garden. The fragrant white blossoms are too familiar to need description. The variety, *L. candidum speciosum* has darker stems and a later flowering period.

Lilium concolor. This dwarf Chinese lily makes an ideal pot plant. It grows from 5-18 inches in height with purple-shaded stems, slender, hairy leaves, and star-like, upright vermilion flowers. Desirable indoors and out.

Lilium davidi. David's lily is an immigrant from Western China, where its habitat is high in the mountains. It has a hairy stem about 40 inches in height covered with narrow leaves, also hairy. Open, nodding flowers—reflexed as a rule —are orange-pink with numerous black spots. Individual flowers are not unlike those of *L. tigrinum,* but are more graceful and delicate in every part. Very hardy and useful in the outdoor garden. *Lilium willmottiae* may be grown instead of *L. davidi* in the window garden. There is no object in growing both, however, as they look so much alike; although the latter is a later bloomer than the former.

Lilium elegans. A group of low-growing lilies of Japanese origin. Although they are universally catalogued as *Lilium elegans,* the group, technically speaking, comprises numerous forms of *Lilium davuricum,* subspecies *thunbergianum.* The flowers are erect and range in color from pale yellow through various shades of orange and red to deep mahogany. The plants grow from 6-14 inches in height and are very hardy and disease-resistant. Many named varieties are on the market.

Lilium japonicum. A fragrant species from Japan. The flowers are horizontal or nearly so, up to 6 inches across, and colored from delicate pink to rose.

Lilium medeoloides. Another Japanese lily, called in its native country Kuruma-yuri; in English bearing the common name of wheel lily due to the leaf-whorls on flower stalks. Not the prettiest of lilies, but an excellent subject for the window garden. 1-6 nodding flowers are carried on stems up to 20 inches in height. The blossoms are apricot to bright scarlet in color, spotted and speckled with black.

Lilium ochraceum. This species comes from Burma and South China. It is quite similar in appearance to *L. nepal-*

ense, and is often catalogued under that name; although the true nepal lily is not in cultivation as far as I know. The plant is recommended as an oddity, not for beauty. Flowers are nodding, mostly green in color, with dark red centers and red dots and markings.

Lilium rubescens. A lily from the west coast of North America, bearing the common names of redwood and chaparral lily. It is not unlike *L. washingtonianum* in appearance and coloring, except the flower-trumpet is narrower and the segments overlap. Flowers are pale lilac when they open first, later becoming rosy-purple, dotted with deeper purple. This is a difficult lily in the outdoor garden but exquisite as a pot plant.

Lilium speciosum. A widely grown Japanese species of great beauty. Reflexed flowers of the type are white, heavily suffused with carmine-pink and profusely dotted with rose-red. Interior of the segments is peppered with varicolored, fleshy papillae. A number of varieties are available in the trade.

L. s. album.	white
L. s. kraetzeri	white, tinged with green on back of petals.
L. s. rubrum	carmine-pink.
L. s. melpomene	deeper carmine-pink.
L. s. magnificum	crimson, with pink spots.

Lilium sulphureum. A trumpet-flowered species from Burma. Flowers are sulphur-yellow inside, exteriors streaked with red.

Lilium tenuifolium. The little coral lily is a great garden favorite as well as being one of the best species for use as a pot plant. It is native to Korea, China, and Siberia, and is very hardy in every respect. It grows from 14-20 inches high with narrow, grass-like leaves, and numerous small, nodding flowers of deep coral-red. This lily may be grown from seed easily and rapidly. The variety, Golden Gleam, grows taller and has flowers of yellow to orange.

Lilium testaceum. The nankeen lily looks like an apricot-colored madonna lily, and is handled in the same manner, i. e. shallow planting. Flowers are more reflexed than those of *L. candidum* and number from 2-10.

Lilium washingtonianum. A native plant of the Pacific Coast, from Oregon to central California. The type has white flowers, but the purple-flowered plant sold usually under the above name is *L. washingtonianum purpureum,* a variety. It is a beautiful thing; difficult to establish in the garden, yet amenable in the house. Tall-growing, 3-6 feet, with few or numerous flowers which open white with purple dots that spread gradually and flush the whole flower a deep purple.

CULTURE: *"Lilies do well in pots. They should be planted in deep, fairly wide receptacles and not crowded too closely together. The large bulbs should have five square inches of space and the small ones two. I planted three tigrinums, which are medium sized bulbs, in a pot measuring nine inches in height and ten inches across the top, and in the same sized pot four elegans, which are small. Three in one pot are leafier and look less like lone toothpicks than one or

* Helen M. Fox, *Garden Cinderellas,* by permission the Macmillan Co., publishers.

even two. Every pot must have a hole in the bottom of it for drainage. Before filling them with soil a few lumps of charcoal, placed on either side and over the hole, will help the drainage and aid in keeping the soil sweet. The soil, made up of two parts compost or topsoil and one part sand, is filled in to a depth of four or five inches and the bulb placed on this and only just covered. More soil is added as the shoot grows until the pot is filled to within one inch of the top. This is done to force the bulb to grow basal roots before the stem roots.

"The pots filled with hardy lilies can be wintered in well-drained cold frames standing on coal ashes or gravel and covered with rotted leaves or hay.

"The more delicate species which otherwise we would have to relinquish altogether smile at us safely from their movable homes if they are wintered in the cellar along with the hydrangeas and oleanders."

For earlier flowering, plant the bulbs in September, bury the pots out of doors until the containers are full of roots, then bring inside and force in a cool location.

LITTONIA

A group of 10 or more species of tuberous, climbing, lily-flowered plants; mostly from Africa. Littonia is closely related to gloriosa, and shares with the latter genus its common name of climbing lily. The chief difference between the two genera lies in the flowers. While blossoms of both are six-parted, the flowers of gloriosa are reflexed; those of littonia are not.

Littonia has lance-shaped, glossy leaves that terminate in tendrils which support the plants as they climb to about 8 feet above the curiously formed tubers.

But few known species are in cultivation. The best one for use as a house or greenhouse plant is described below.

DESCRIPTION: *Littonia modesta,* var. *keiti.* The flowers are orange in color, bell-shaped, nodding, about 1-1½ inches across, and are not reflexed. The lower leaves occur in 3's; upper leaves are alternate and tipped with tendrils.

CULTURE: Identical with gloriosa, which see.

ORNITHOGALUM

ORNITHOGALUM

A genus of the lily family containing about 70 species of hardy and tender bulbous herbs native to Europe, Asia, and Africa. Hardy ornithogalums are grown in the garden and are inclined to become pests due to their prolific increase. On the other hand, the tender species, mostly African in habitat, make long-lasting and lovely house plants. Ornithogalum grows from quite small true bulbs. Leaves are narrow or broad, according to species, and are pointed at the tip. Flowers are borne in racemes on leafless stalks up to 3 feet in height, above small leafy bracts. Blossoms in this genus are noted for their long life when cut.

DESCRIPTION: *Ornithogalum arabicum.* A semi-hardy species with small white flowers whose petal bases are inked in black. Intensely fragrant in the outdoor garden, and some of the odor is retained in house-grown plants.

Ornithogalum maculatum. A small species with orange flowers. The three outer petals bear spots or blotches of a darker color.

Ornithogalum saundersoni. A very large ornithogalum with pure white flowers.

Ornithogalum splendens. Another large species with flamboyant clusters of brilliant orange-red flowers.

Ornithogalum thyrsoides. This is the so-called wonder flower due to the long life of its blossoms. The buds are flushed with yellow, and open to white or primrose.

Ornithogalum thyrsoides aureum. A lovely form of *O. thyrsoides* with flowers of golden-yellow.

Ornithogalum thunbergianum. One of the large, tender species with orange-shaded, yellow flowers.

CULTURE: Plant the bulbs in August or September, as an early start is essential to healthy growth. Fill pots with a soil mixture consisting of: three-fifths rich soil; one-fifth sharp sand; one-fifth old cow manure. Place the containers in a cool cellar or cold frame until roots show through the drainage holes. Then grow in a cool room where the temperature is 55-65 degrees for flowering. Flowers may be expected from January through April according to species planted and age of bulbs. The technique of forcing ornithogalums is similar to indoor freesia culture.

ROHDEA

A genus of the lily family from Japan containing one species. It is a tender foliage plant resembling aspidistra, with leaves 1-2 feet long. Small, creamy-white flowers are borne on short, thick spikes only a few inches high and hidden among the leaves. The flowers are followed later by large red berries which hold their color for many months.

DESCRIPTION: *Rohdea japonica.* Grows from a long, cylindrical rootstock with fleshy fibers. Flowers are described above. The narrow, erect leaves are produced in a rosette. They are 9-12 in number. Many named varieties of the type are available which differ in shape and color of the leaves; flowers are similar throughout.

CULTURE: Plant in regular lily potting mixture. Place the rootstock just under the surface of the soil. Water sparingly at first, then handle as you would pandanus or aspidistra. No resting period required.

SANDERSONIA

A South African genus, seldom seen in the window garden anywhere. The beautiful orange, bell-shaped flowers are called Christmas bells.

DESCRIPTION: *Sandersonia aurantiaca.* Grows from a tuberous rootstock. The leaves are lance-shaped or linear. Flowers are solitary and occur in upper leaf-axils; they are globe-like in shape.

CULTURE: The same as for ornithogalum, except regular lily potting mixture is used.

SCHIZOBASOPSIS

(*synonym, Bowiea*)

Little can be said about the beauty of this strange South African bulbous plant, *Schizobasopsis volubilis*. Yet it is a curious and interesting addition to a window garden collection. From the very large bulb arises a heavily branched, deep green stem bearing a few scaly leaves which soon drop off. Later, greenish-white flowers are carried on the tangled stems. Probably the most interesting thing about this odd plant is the fact that it represents one of the most drought-resistant vegetative growths known.

CULTURE: Use a typical cactus potting mixture of: two parts sand; two parts ground brick; two parts ground limestone; two parts loam; one half part peat moss; one handful of bone meal. Dry the bulb off during the summer, out of the pot; and repot in the fall for winter growth. Grow in a dry atmosphere and water sparingly.

TRICYRTIS

A genus of about 9 species of perennial herbs from Formosa and Japan. Two species are in cultivation, one of which is a not uncommon garden plant known as the toad

Brodiaea uniflora. Page 121

Lilium speciosum. Page 140

STUD PINK (*Helonias bullata*). Page 133

THE WONDER FLOWER (*Ornithogalum thyrsoides*).

lily. The name is most unprepossesing, but the plant is not. Summer-flowering.

DESCRIPTION: *Tricyrtis hirta.* The toad lily grows from a thick rootstock to a height of about 3 feet. Leaves are alternate and oval, 4-6 inches long. The 1 inch flowers are white, spotted inside with black and purple. They occur in small clusters, or singly, in leaf axils.

TRICYRTIS

Tricyrtis macropoda. Same size as above species but flowers are smaller (¾ inch) and bell-shaped. They are light purple in color, spotted inside, and they are borne in terminal clusters.

CULTURE: Plant in regular lily potting mixture and handle like lilies; except the plants should be dried off gradually in late autumn and the rootstocks kept in dry storage over winter.

VELTHEIMIA

Another South African genus, as yet rare in indoor gardens but becoming increasingly popular due to ease of culture and satisfactory flowering. It blooms in early spring. The flower spikes resemble those of a red hot poker plant (Kniphofia) but are daintier in coloring and appearance. Additional plants may be obtained from offsets, seeds, and leaves.

DESCRIPTION: *Veltheimia glauca.* Grows from a large tunicated bulb. Leaves are oblong-strap-shaped, from 8-12 inches in length, and somewhat curled and crisped. The mottled flower stalk is 12-18 inches in height, round and stout. The flower spike is dense, 3-6 inches long; and individual, tubular flowers are about 1 inch long. The color is coral-pink.

Veltheimia viridifolia. Grows from a large tunicated bulb. Not unlike the above species but is a little larger, and flower stamens do not protrude from the tube as in *V. glauca.* Flowers are yellow or tinted with pink. The leaves of this species are exceptionally brilliant green.

CULTURE: The same as for amaryllis, including amaryllis potting mixture.

VI

OTHER PLANTS

Chapter 6

OTHER PLANTS

THIS CHAPTER is devoted to a miscellany of plants from many families and countries. The material listed is all excellent for potting and growing indoors; yet there are too few species and varieties in each family group to warrant a family chapter similar to that given the amaryllids, aroids, irids, and members of the Liliaceae. In making this selection from a variety of family groups, I have included only *available* species and hybrids, of course.

There are a number of subjects here included that offer a gamut of bizarre, beautiful, or just plain satisfactory window garden plants. Some are of easiest culture; others are more difficult to handle. All, however, may be grown in the house under average conditions, with few exceptions. Where special treatment is indicated, it will be described together with the plant; for little or no general information can be expressed about the plants in this chapter. They are too cosmopolitan in habitat, character, and culture; and must be considered separately.

ACHIMENES

family, Gesneriaceae

Tropical American bulbous plants with showy, gloxinia-like flowers. Achimenes grows from a rhizome, and as a house plant may be grown in hanging containers or ordinary pots. While about 40 species are known, only 2 or 3 are in cultivation, and they are seldom grown as there are numerous named hybrids available which are superior in every way to the species. Summer-flowering.

The following information about the genus was published in "Horticulture" by a successful grower. With thanks to the Massachusetts Horticultural Society it is reprinted herewith.

"Many persons who have tried to grow achimenes never have been successful. Therefore, a few cultural notes on growing these indispensable summer-flowering plants may be timely.

"Achimenes is a native of tropical America, and is very closely allied to gesneria, tydaea, and gloxinia, and consequently it needs a warm house or greenhouse in which to start. A temperature of 60 degrees Fahrenheit at night suits it best.

"It is a common practice to plant the little rhizomes in the pots or pans where they are intended to flower. This, I think, is largely the cause of the failures and disappointments heard about. It is far better to start the rhizomes in shallow boxes in a mixture of equal parts of leaf-soil and sand. Care should be taken not to cover them too deeply.

Then place them in the warmest part of the house or green-house, with shade and a little moisture. Growth should appear in about two weeks. When the plants are one to two inches high, they can then be transplanted into the kind of receptacle desired. The choice of hanging baskets, pots, or pans depends upon how and where they are to be used after coming into bloom. Be liberal with the plants no matter what they are planted in. Use 18 to 24 in an eight inch pan.

"For final potting I prefer a light sod loam with a small amount of leaf-soil and sand to make it loose and open. To this may also be added a four inch pot of Scotch soot and a six inch pot of sheep manure to every wheelbarrowful of compost. After the plants have been transplanted, the utmost care should be taken not to let them become bone dry, since a single drying may ruin the plants completely. Keep them moist but not soaking wet. Water only with lukewarm water until the plants are established.

"The achimenes vary greatly in growth and habits. Some grow much taller than others. In that case it is advisable to pinch back by removing the very center growth when they are four or five inches tall. At this time it is well to give them some support, but to stake every individual plant in the pot is far from satisfactory. I prefer birch brush, selecting only the very slender shoots about 8 inches high, placing them all through the middle of the pot as well as around the outer edge. This will do away with all further staking or support, and when the plants come into flower, the brush will never be seen, and the plant will look loose and natural.

"Manure water is very beneficial and can be given about twice weekly when the plants come into bud. Avoid all artificial fertilizers. Remember to keep a light shade over the plants at all times.

"Achimenes can be kept in flower from May to October and later if one desires, by starting a late batch of rhizomes. For summer-flowering we start them in March or April. They will then bloom continuously all summer, and will do well on the sun porch or piazza, providing they are protected from strong sunshine and high winds.

"There are many varieties in commerce today, but the so-called hybrids introduced in recent years are used almost exclusively, because they surpass the older sorts both in color and size of flower. We have still with us, however, two of the older varieties which we think are worth grow-ing—the Margarita, pure white with a yellow eye; and the Ambrose Verschaffelt, white veined with lilac.

"The newer varieties I would recommend are the follow-ing: Dainty Queen, large pure white flowers with pink eye; Galatea Improved, large deep lavender flowers; Magnifica, violet-blue; Purity, pure white (entirely white); Purple King, rich purple; Supreme, lavender with a light center; Gloria, violet-blue; Swansoni, basic color, mauve, mottled with blue and with a white throat; Orchidee, cattleya-pink; Achievement, rose-pink with a carmine eye."

ALLOPLECTUS

family, Gesneriaceae

A genus of tender, tropical, evergreen plants containing 30 or more species, a few of which are in cultivation and useful in the house for their colorful foliage and showy, tubular flowers which are borne in the leaf axils. The plants grow from tuberous roots and are summer-flowering.

DESCRIPTION: *Alloplectus repens.* This is a trailing species, creeping by means of roots projected between the pairs of leaves. The leaves are oval, toothed, and may be either hairy or smooth. The gaping, tubular flowers are yellow, tinged with red.

Alloplectus schlimi. A sub-shrub with 3-4 inch oval leaves, green above and purplish on the under side. The flowers are red and yellow.

Alloplectus sparsiflorus. An erect plant with leafstalks and the under side of leaves marked and veined in red. The flowers have purple sepals and a yellow, club-shaped corolla.

CULTURE: Pot alloplectus tubers in February or early March in a soil mixture consisting of: two parts loam; one part sand; one part leaf mold; one-half part old cow manure; and a generous amount of bone meal. New plants should be shaded from the sun and kept in a humid atmosphere of 70-80 degrees temperature. Rest after flowering by drying off, then store the tubers in a dark location at about 40 degrees. Water frequently during the growing season and supply manure water every two or three weeks.

BILLBERGIA

family, Bromeliaceae

A genus of tree-perching plants from Tropical America. Of these epiphytes less than 50 species are known, and 2 only are in general cultivation. Both of these species make excellent house or greenhouse plants. The leaves are spiny, reminiscent of pineapple foliage. They are produced in basal rosettes, and from these arise the tall, branched flower stalks.

DESCRIPTION: *Billbergia nutans.* Most widely grown bromeliad in the genus. Leaves, as described above, are 1-2 feet in length. The flowers appear in long, branching clusters, 4-8 blossoms in each group. They are green in color, edged with blue, and from each protrude 6 long stamens with yellow anthers. Below each flower cluster are handsome, deep pink bracts.

Billbergia rubro-cyanea. This species is quite similar to *B. nutans,* but is larger. Another difference is that the bracts subtending the flower clusters are glowing scarlet instead of pink.

CULTURE: Potting mixture for billbergia should be one-half chopped fern roots (osmunda) and one-half a mixture of: two parts loam; one part leaf mold; one part sand; and a handful of bone meal. The plants may be grown in pots, yet better results are attained by suspending this epiphyte in hanging baskets or orchid cribs. If pots are used as containers, double the usual amount of drainage material. Use less water when the plants are budded and in flower. The growing temperature should be between 70 and 80 degrees accompanied by high humidity where possible. No resting period is required. Supply lots of water during the active growing period (spring and summer) prior to budding and flowering.

BORONIA

family, Rutaceae

A genus of evergreen, Australian sub-shrubs noted for their fragrance. Leaves are opposite and compound. The flowers occur along stems, either singly or doubly, and are very numerous. The aromatic characteristics of this genus justify its use in the house; and the exceptional abundance of blossoms may be considered as a bonus.

DESCRIPTION: *Boronia megastigma.* A small, twiggy plant growing from 1-2 feet in height. Leaves are less than an inch in length. The flowers, about ½ inch wide, are purple outside and yellow within.

CULTURE: Plant in a potting mixture of: three parts sand; two parts loam; two parts peat moss; two parts leaf mold; one-half part old cow manure. Keep anything containing lime away from plants in this genus. Water sparingly and supply when necessary only. After blooming, cut the plants to the soil. Replacement of plants will be necessary every two or three years. No resting period required.

BRUCKENTHALIA

family, Ericaceae

A beautiful, small, heath-like shrub; the only species in this genus. It is quite hardy in character and may be found growing in rock gardens as far north as southern New England. At the same time it makes a splendid pot plant everywhere.

DESCRIPTION: *Bruckenthalia spiculifolia.* The little spike heath grows to about 10 inches in height. The leaves are very short and narrow but exceedingly numerous and dense upon the branches. Flowers are pink in color, bell-shaped, about ¼ inch long, and are carried in short spikes; clusters which seldom reach to 1 inch in length.

CULTURE: The same as for brunfelsia, but add a handful of coarse gravel to the mixture in each pot. Like all members of the heath family, bruckenthalia is most intolerant of anything containing lime. The plant, being moderately hardy, should be grown in the lower temperature range, 60-65 degrees. Water only when the need is indicated.

BRUNFELSIA

family, Solanaceae

A group of Tropical American shrubs and trees of the potato family. While several species are in cultivation, one in particular is grown in greenhouses and conservatories for the exquisite scent of its flowers. The plant is probably too large for most window gardens, yet where space is available its presence will be enjoyed thoroughly.

DESCRIPTION: *Brunfelsia americana.* The lady-of-the-night normally grows to a height of 6 feet or a little taller. By keeping the plant rootbound and pruned it may be maintained at a much smaller stature. As a matter of fact, brunfelsia flowers much better when its roots *are* potbound. Leaves are about 3 inches long and oval in shape. The flowers are tubular, 3-4 inches long, and intensely fragrant, particularly after dark. They open white and fade gradually to pale yellow. The fruit is yellow and about the size of a marble.

CULTURE: This plant should be potted or tubbed in equal parts of loam, peat moss, and sand, to which has been added a little leaf mold and old cow manure. Do not use bone meal or any fertilizer containing lime; and do not grow in a temperature of less than 60 degrees. Watering may be reduced a little a month after flowering.

CALATHEA

family, Marantaceae

A genus of handsome foliage plants containing 100 or more species from Tropical America, mostly; although a few are native to Tropical Africa. Many calatheas, sold as such, actually are marantas, a closely allied genus differing only in certain technical characteristics.

Leaves, for which the plants are grown, are beautifully marked and variegated in shades of red, brown, yellow, green, and white. They are not unlike fancy-leaved caladiums in appearance, but are stouter, and the leafstalk is attached at the bottom of the leafblade instead of at the center as it is in caladium.

The flowers are not striking in size or beauty; for that matter seldom appearing at all on specimens grown in the window garden. Calathea grows from a rootstock or rhizome.

DESCRIPTION: There are so many calatheas (or marantas catalogued as calatheas) available that space is lacking for a detailed listing. In addition to the few described herewith, you will find the following (and other) calatheas offered for sale in various dealers' catalogues and price lists: *bachemiana, chimboracensis, crotalifera, eximia, fasciata, lageriana, legrelliana, medio-picta, nitens, princeps, pulchella, smaragdina, tubispatha, vandenheckei, veitchiana, virginalis, warscewiczi, wiotiana.*

Calathea bicolor (Maranta bicolor). A small plant growing to about 1 foot in height. The elliptic leaves have wavy margins: they are blue-green on the upper side, purple below. Also there is a pale band along the midrib. Its native habitat is Brazil.

Calathea lietzei (Maranta conspicua). The leaves in this species are oval-lanceolate, heart-shaped at the base. The upper surfaces are brilliant green, with areas of darker green; purple beneath. Brazil.

Calathea makoyana (Maranta olivaris). Grows to 3 feet in height. The broad leaves are blotched, olive-green above, and red below. Brazil.

Calathea ornata, also sold by dealers as *Calathea sanderiana,* and regarded by botanists as *Maranta rosea lineata.* Grows 1½-3 feet in height and is one of the best species in cultivation. The leaves are 1-2 feet long, green above and purple beneath in older plants. In young plants the leaves usually are streaked between veins with white and pink. There are a number of named horticultural varieties of this northern South American plant available, with various types and patterns of leaf-coloring.

Calathea roseo-picta. One of the smallest species; height about 8 inches. The 6 inch, nearly round leaves are green above, ribbed and blotched with red; purplish beneath. Brazil.

Calathea zebrina (*Maranta zebrina*). The most commonly cultivated species. Height, 1½-3 feet. Leaves up to 20 inches in length. Upper leaf surfaces are soft green, veins and mid-ribs barred with yellow-green and very dark green; under side of leaves are purple-red. Brazil.

CULTURE: The same as for arum, which see.

CANARINA

family, Campanulaceae

Bulbous tropical herbs from the Canary Islands, closely allied to the genus *Campanula;* but with calyx and corolla tubes grown together.

DESCRIPTION: *Canarina campanulata.* Grows from a tuberous root. Solitary, bell-shaped flowers of yellow, flushed with purple-brown and veined with the same color. Each flower is about 1½ inches wide and 1 inch long. The buds are decorative, being saccate and drooping.

Canarina emini. Grows from a tuberous root. A smaller species with blossoms of brilliant scarlet.

CULTURE: Plant the roots, as soon as purchased, in amaryllis potting mixture with additional drainage material. Moisten the soil and place the pot, or pots, in a warm, dark place for two weeks. Then bring into the light and water frequently. After flowering, rest the plants but supply enough water to keep the tubers plump and healthy. Growing temperature, 60-70 degrees: resting temperature, 40-50 degrees.

As a house plant canarina is not very long-lived, and it may be necessary to buy new roots every year or every other year. However, if you enjoy the plant, annual renewal is inexpensive.

CARICA

family, Caricaceae

The pawpaw is a Tropical American fruit tree of considerable importance. Male and female flowers are produced on different trees, usually. The staminate flowers are yellow, funnel-shaped, fragrant, and carried in long-stalked clusters. Pistillate blossoms are 5-petalled, almost stalkless, and yellow also. Seedling trees make good house plants. There is no need of discussing the fruit; for there will be none on window garden specimens; although fruiting is possible in a greenhouse.

DESCRIPTION: *Carica papaya.* Should be grown from seed for house plant use. The 7-lobed leaves are interesting; they turn downward as leafstalks lengthen, and eventually screen the stalk or trunk of the plant.

C. papaya increases in size rapidly and will outgrow its welcome in three or four years, probably. Seedling avocadoes, or alligator pears, are grown in many window gardens. Pawpaw may be considered as a parallel example of the use of tree seedlings for pot plants.

CULTURE: Plant the seeds in lily potting mixture, keep moist always, and give plenty of sun. No special care is necessary, yet do not let the plants get touched by frost if you decide to plunge them in the garden during the summer months.

GINGER LILY (*Hedychium gardnerianum*). Page 169

ACHIMENES. Page 152

FIRE-THORN (*Pyracantha duvalli*). Page 188

SWEET OLIVE (*Osmanthus fragrans*). Page 183

CISSUS

family, Vitaceae

A genus of mostly tropical vines resembling grape vines except there are technical differences and the fruit is inedible. A few species are cultivated for their fine foliage and are grown in the house or greenhouse. All climb by tendrils, and the nondescript flowers are small and 4-petaled. Most members of the genus are suitable for greenhouse culture only; yet there are two species which are invaluable in the house window garden or elsewhere.

DESCRIPTION: *Cissus antarctica.* Commonly called the kangaroo vine. The leaves are glossy, dark green, and deeply toothed: they are oval or heart-shaped and about 4 inches in length. The plant may be kept pruned in compact bush form, or allowed to ramble as a vine.

Cissus striata. A low, shrubby vine with hairy, evergreen, compound leaves of 3-5 leaflets from 1-3 inches long and toothed. *C. striata* may be kept in control easily. This is a fine plant for the kitchen window or windows.

CULTURE: The best potting mixture for cissus is: two parts loam; two parts sand; two parts leaf mold; one-half part old cow manure; and a tablespoonful of bone meal to each pot. Buy young plants and grow them along in normal house temperature with ample water and a little sun. Spray occasionally and dose with manure water once a month. No resting period required. Watch out for scale, mealybug, and red spider. Spraying with water will control these pests as a rule. If not, use insecticides.

CLERODENDRON

family, Verbenaceae

A large genus of vines, shrubs, and trees, mostly tropical in habitat, of the verbena family. Of the several cultivated clerodendrons, one in particular makes an exquisite plant for the house or greenhouse.

DESCRIPTION: *Clerodendron thomsonae.* A woody, shrubby vine of great beauty, commonly called bag-flower. The leaves are ovalish, opposite, sometimes lobed, and 2½-4½ inches long. Flowers are most unusual. They have 5 crimson segments in the corolla which is ½ inch across, with 4 long curving stamens. The calyx is white or creamy, about ¾ of an inch long, and shaped like a miniature Japanese lantern. Blossoms are borne in clusters; they appear in late spring and continue to flower most of the summer.

CULTURE: Plant in lily potting mixture and grow in a cool temperature, 60-68 degrees. Water regularly, and the plants do better when humidity is rather high. No resting period is required. Propagation is by means of cuttings made from new wood.

C. thomsonae may be kept pruned in compact form, or allowed to climb upon a support. In either instance it will be a most pleasing addition to any indoor collection.

CONANDRON

family, Gesneriaceae

A rare little tuberous-rooted herb from the mountains of Japan, with 6-12 white, or purple, nodding flowers whose shape suggests that of the blossoms of dodecatheon. Very seldom grown as a house plant, yet merits a place in any window garden collection. The leaves are rough and toothed, oblong in shape.

DESCRIPTION: *Conandron ramondioides.* Grows to about 10 inches in height. Numerous glossy, crinkly leaves and little reflexed flowers of purple, with yellow eyes.

CULTURE: Conandron may be grown from seed or roots. Use regular amaryllis potting mixture to which add a pinch of aluminum sulphate to insure a soil on the acid side. Grow in good light but keep away from direct sun. Water frequently after growth has started. After blooming, rest the plant in the cellar. Do not allow soil in the pot to become dust dry during the dormant period.

CORYTHOLOMA

family, Gesneriaceae

A sizable genus of tuberous-rooted, Tropical American herbs related to gesneria and more distantly to gloxinia. The flowers, which appear in spring, have long, and often curved, tubes. Upper lips are helmet-shaped. The few species in cultivation make showy and amenable house plants.

DESCRIPTION: *Corytholoma cardinalis.* Grows about 1 foot high with hairy stems. The leaves are wavy-toothed, oval or heart-shaped, and from 4-6 inches long. Flowers are red, 2-2¾ inches in length, and occur either in leaf axils or clustered at the top of the stalk.

Corytholoma warscewiczi. This Mexican species has tubular flowers of orange and scarlet. Otherwise it is quite similar to *C. cardinalis*.

CULTURE: The same as for alloplectus, but pot the tubers in late fall or early winter. When tubers are not available, corytholoma may be grown from seed without difficulty; just a longer wait for flowers. In watering plants allied to gloxinia keep away from the leaves; they spot and rot very easily.

CRYPTANTHUS

family, Bromeliaceae

A genus of tree-perching bromeliads from South America. Several of the 12 or more species are useful in the house or greenhouse for their foliage and flowers. The leaves are stiff, with spiny margins, and are produced in basal rosettes. White flowers are produced in dense heads right in the middle of the leaf clusters. Summer-flowering in the house or greenhouse.

DESCRIPTION: *Cryptanthus acaulis*. The 6-12 spiny leaves are about 1 inch wide and 4-5 inches long. They are green on the upper surface and mealy-white below.

Cryptanthus zonatus. A handsomer plant than the above species and larger in all its parts. The leaves are boldly banded in white or brown; and the entire leafblade sometimes has a pinkish cast.

CULTURE: The potting mixture should consist of: two parts loam; one part leaf mold; one part sand; one-half part old cow manure; and osmunda fiber equal in bulk to all other ingredients. Grow in a temperature of 50-65 degrees. Active growth begins in March or early April at which time supply plenty of water, less after November when the dormant season starts. Cryptanthus may be grown in hanging baskets, or pots.

CYPHOMANDRA

family, Colanaceae

A South American genus closely related to the tomatoes; in fact one species bears the name of tree tomato, due to brown, egg-shaped fruits which follow the small, pinkish flowers.

The genus comprises 30 or more species of herbs, shrubs, and trees; one of which makes a splendid large tub plant—where there is space to use it.

DESCRIPTION: *Cyphomandra betacea.* Tree tomato. Normally grows to 10 feet, but is much smaller as a tub plant. The heart-shaped leaves are hairy and from 8-12 inches in length. Small clusters of pinkish flowers are produced in the leaf axils, followed by the smooth, acid-tasting fruit. This Brazilian plant is not of primary importance as a house plant; yet it is an interesting subject for out-of-the-ordinary indoor plant collections.

CULTURE: Use regular lily potting mixture. Replace soil annually, water regularly, and give the tree tomato manure water after buds have formed. Sun is not essential, but helps in forming the fruits which are edible—either you will like them or think they are impossible! Prune when necessary to keep in control, and watch out for red spider.

EPISCIA

family, Gesneriaceae

A Tropical American genus of 30 or more species characterized by the hairy leaves and drooping tendencies. Slender, branching stems arise from creeping roots or rhizomes which may, or may not be, branched. The leaves are unequal, opposite, hairy above and reddish on the under side. They are oval in shape, or nearly round, with scalloped margins. Flowers are scarlet mostly, although in some species they are purple; white in others. The blossoms occur singly or clustered in the leaf axils. They are saccate, with straight or curved tubes and about ¾ of an inch wide. At least one species is available and there may be others which I have failed to discover.

DESCRIPTION: *Episcia cupreata.* A slender species with trailing habits. Flowers are scarlet and quite showy; yet the plant is grown for its soft, hairy leaves and the coppery bands which border midribs of the leaves.

CULTURE: The same as for alloplectus, but episcia may be grown at lower temperatures if there is sufficient humidity in the growing location.

ERYTHRINA

family, Leguminosae

A large tropical genus of trees, shrubs, and herbaceous plants of the pea family. The leaves, mostly, are compound with 3 broad leaflets. Flowers, which are produced in dense or loose racemes, are various shades of red in color and very showy. The individual blossoms are pea-flower-like in shape. The plants are spiny and very rapid growers. But very few members of this group are in general cultivation.

DESCRIPTION: *Erythrina crista-galli.* Grows from a fleshy rootstock. A Brazilian shrub or small tree, called coral tree, which sometimes grows 10-14 feet in height; at other times it develops a very short trunk and remains dwarf in stature. As a rule the branches die back after flowering. Stems and leafstalks are somewhat spiny. Of the erythrina species and varieties in cultivation, this species is the best for use as a winter-flowering tub plant. The loose clusters of flowers are brilliant crimson.

CULTURE: Use lily potting mixture and repeated applications of liquid manure as the plant is a heavy feeder. Grow in a moderately cool location and water frequently. After flowering, the roots appreciate a vacation for 60 days; yet apply enough moisture from time to time to prevent them from becoming noticeably desiccated. Erythrina makes a splendid outdoor plant in the southern states.

HEDYCHIUM

family, Zingiberaceae

A genus of interesting herbs from the warmer sections of Asia, colloquially called ginger lilies. As a matter of fact these plants are allied closely to true ginger, differing only in a few botanical technicalities. The large, base-sheathed leaves are clean and bright, and add greatly to the attractiveness of the plants. Showy, bracted flowers are borne in ter-

minal clusters in late fall or early winter. Plants in this genus
grow from tuberous rootstocks.

Numerous hedychium varieties are obtainable as well as
the several species listed below.

DESCRIPTION: *Hedychium chrysoleucum.* A large plant
from India, 2½-5 feet in height. Leaves are about 4 inches
wide and vary in length from 1 foot to just under 2 feet.
The red flowers are touched with orange-yellow at the base
of the lips.

Hedychium coronarium. This is the species most generally grown. It is quite large, growing to 7 feet out of doors,
much smaller as a pot plant. Leaves are 1-3 feet in length
and 3-5 inches wide. The intensely fragrant flowers are
white, 1½-3 inches long. Occasionally, lower lips of the
flowers show a blush of yellow. The species is native to
Tropical Asia.

Hedychium gardnerianum. A magnificent plant growing
to 6 feet in the garden. Leaves are shorter and broader than
in the two species described above. The 2 inch flowers are
yellow, with protruding stamens of vivid red; and are borne
in spikes up to 18 inches in length. This native of India is
one of the showiest hedychiums. It is not available at all
times; yet recently I have seen it listed, so apparently it is
again being stocked.

CULTURE: Plant the rootstocks in late winter or early spring
in the same potting mixture recommended for alloplectus.
Hedychium needs a warm growing location, humidity, and
lots of water. Applications of manure water should be made
every two weeks, for these plants are heavy feeders. After

flowering, dry the plants off gradually until the leaves have ripened and turned. Then rest the plants in pots for two months. New growth may then be encouraged by copious watering.

ISOLOMA

family, Gesneriaceae

Fifty or more species of tender Tropical American plants growing from rootstocks. They are close relatives of achimenes and gesneria, and require much the same handling. Isoloma leaves are very handsome, being marked in contrasting colors and, in most species, covered with downy hairs. The tubular flowers have asymmetrical lips and appear in axils of the leaves, either singly or severally: at times they occur in leafy terminal clusters.

Several species and numerous hybrids are on the market, mostly with red to orange flowers variously dotted and marked with purple.

Isoloma is seen growing in greenhouses occasionally; seldom is it to be found in window gardens, although it is just as satisfactory there as are gloxinia and other gesneriads.

DESCRIPTION: *Isoloma amabile.* A Colombian isoloma growing 1-2½ feet in height. The stalked leaves are ovalish in shape and deeply toothed. Leaf-veins are purple, and irregular purple patches lend color to the leafblades. The flowers are dark red, blotched and dotted with purple: the inside of the flower tube is lighter in color than the exterior.

Isoloma hirsutum. This is a very hairy species native to

the West Indies. The plant is larger than *I. amabile,* growing as high as 4 feet—smaller, however, in pots. Flowers
are nodding, purple in color, and distinctly hairy.

Isoloma hybrida. Under this listing in dealers' catalogues
are a number of unnamed hybrid isolomas; all worth growing.

CULTURE: Follow instructions given for alloplectus, but
grow at a little higher temperature, and include one extra
part of leaf mold in the potting mixture.

IXORA

family, Rubiaceae

This genus comprises a group of Tropical Asiatic shrubs.
They are grown out of doors in Florida and California; in
other states ixora is useful only in the greenhouse, conservatory, or window garden as it is far too tender to survive
the open garden. As young plants, several species are most
welcome additions to a house plant collection. If there is
room to grow the shrubs on as tub plants, you may look
forward to years of cheerful colorful company.

DESCRIPTION: *Ixora coccinea.* The jungle geranium is an
evergreen shrub bearing dense clusters of deep red tubular
flowers, 1½-2 inches in length. The leaves are oblong in
shape and quite large, 4-5 inches; and the fruit is a 2-seeded
berry.

Ixora fulgens. This species has narrower leaves than
I. coccinea, and the flowers are orange-scarlet instead of red.
They occur in large stemless bunches. Fruit is similar to
species above.

The scarletbush, *Hamelia erecta,* is sometimes confused with ixora. It is quite similar, differing principally in fruit construction, yet it is a larger shrub and not as amenable for house plant use.

CULTURE: Ixora does well in a potting mixture of equal parts of good loam, leaf mold, and sand, to which should be added some balanced plant food. Growing temperature should not be below 65 degrees at any time. Humidity is appreciated and no resting period is required.

LEPTOSPERMUM

family, Myrtaceae

An Australasian genus of trees and shrubs comprising about 30 species. While generally bearing the common name of tea tree, the leptospermums are in no way related to the true tea plant. The small leaves are very rigid and almost thorny in appearance. Numerous flowers are produced, either singly or in groups of 2-3 at the ends of short branches or in the leaf axils.

The species described below normally grows to a height of almost 20 feet, yet may be kept reasonably small and compact as a tub plant.

DESCRIPTION: *Leptospermum scoparium,* var. *nichollsi.* The white flowers, which appear on forced plants in early spring, are 5-petalled, about ½ inch across, spurred, and quite round. Leaves are numerous and less than ½ inch long. New growth looks silky.

CULTURE: Similar to erica, the heaths. Potting soil is two

parts leaf mold to one part sand. Plunge pots in the garden during summer months—in full sun—and return to the house in late August. Grow in a very cool location until February or March; then increase the temperature to 60-65 degrees for flowering. Usually the plants are slow growing.

NAEGELIA

family, Gesneriaceae

Another small genus of gesneriads from Tropical America valuable in the window garden for the foliage principally, although the flowers are attractive, too, being tubular and borne in showy terminal clusters. The velvety leaves are opposite, heart-shaped, and have a pleasing soft texture. Plants in this genus grow from tuberous roots.

DESCRIPTION: *Naegelia cinnabarina.* A Mexican species growing to 1½-2 feet in height. The flowers are quite large, 1½ inches long, drooping, red in color with white-spotted throats. Blooms in the winter months.

Naegelia multiflora. Also from Mexico. A smaller species than *N. cinnabarina* with white flowers and long-haired leaves. Blooms in the winter.

Naegelia zebrina. A 2 foot naegelia from Brazil, blooming in the fall. The flowers are red, spotted with yellow. Leaves are very hairy, the veins colored in brown, red, or purple. This is the best and most decorative naegelia for the window garden.

CULTURE: Plant each tuberous root in a 6 inch pot about 1 inch under the soil surface. The potting mixture to use is: one part peat; one part leaf mold; one part rich loam; one-half part old cow manure and sand, mixed. Supply but little water until growth is well under way, then water frequently. Manure water is appreciated every week or so until flowering is over. Then reduce watering and rest the roots for at least two months.

NEPENTHES

family, Nepenthaceae

Old World, insectivorous, pitcher plants. Some are climbers, others are tree-perching epiphytes. While these fascinating plants are by no means the easiest subjects to handle in the house—being primarily greenhouse plants—it can be done with a little extra effort. The extraordinary pitchers produced by all the species and hybrids are worth extended effort to grow and enjoy.

When young, tropical climbing nepenthes have rosettes of leaves growing upon the ground similar to our native pitcher plants (*Sarracenia*). With age, the plants grow higher and higher above the damp soil in which they are rooted until the groping tips come in contact with underbrush, tree limbs, or anything that offers support. Then the plants assume the characteristics of a vine and not infrequently climb to the tree tops.

Leaves terminate in tendrils at the end of which hang the pitchers. As the plant climbs, the tendrils wind about anything with which they come in contact, and in this manner secure the attached pitchers firmly in position.

The bright bowls are sought by insects and other flying creatures; they are attracted by signal patches of color and

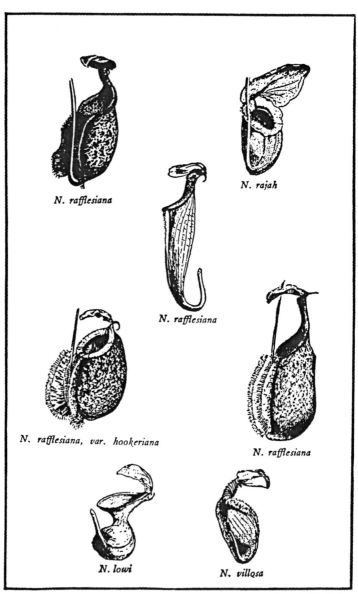

N. rafflesiana

N. rajah

N. rafflesiana

N. rafflesiana, var. hookeriana

N. rafflesiana

N. lowi

N. villosa

PITCHERS OF VARIOUS NEPENTHES

Several illustrations of *Nepenthes rafflesiana* pitchers are used to show how shapes may vary in the same species. As a rule, the higher on the plant pitchers are formed, the more cylindrical they become.

the supply of honey secreted by epidermal cells on the under surface of pitcher lids, and upon the mouth of each pitcher.

Seekers of nectar from the lips of nepenthes wander carelessly near the glossy waxen throat of a pitcher, slip, and fall into the pool of liquid to be found in each trap. Some victims perish at once; others try to climb out of the pitfall, but face glassy-smooth walls and down-pointing teeth which effectively prevent escape.

The liquid in these pitchers is most interesting. It originates from special gland-cells on the inner surface of the pitcher, is mostly water, and as long as there is nothing in the trap gives a very weak acid reaction. However, as soon as a subject is caught, more fluid is excreted which has the ability to dissolve albuminous material such as flesh and blood. It corresponds to gastric juices in the human stomach and reacts in the same manner. Thus are nepenthes victims absorbed by the plant.

Nepenthes pitchers vary in size. Small species produce vegetative traps a fraction of an inch in height. One of the Borneo nepenthes has pitchers large enough to digest a squirrel.

Growers interested in nepenthes have produced many fine hybrids with magnificent pitchers. It is impractical to list the species and hybrids here, for they are legion, and availability varies from time to time.

The safest method to use in acquiring one or more specimens of nepenthes for house use is to visit a greenhouse where they are grown for sale. Choose the plant or plants desired, take them home, and provide required growing conditions as closely as possible. Experience with the genus may lead to experiments in growing, propagating, and even hybridizing; yet do not try this until you have learned something about the idiosyncrasies and requirements of nepenthes. On the other hand, healthy greenhouse-grown specimens may be depended upon to furnish months of pleasure. Any house plant grower may well take pride in the ownership of these unique and highly specialized carnivorous plants.

CULTURE: As a rule, hybrid nepenthes are easier to grow in the house than are the species. If the greenhouse has not provided containers and potting mixtures, plant nepenthes in a pot or orchid crib in equal parts of fibrous peat, rich garden loam, and osmunda or chopped fern roots. If a pot is used, mix two handfuls of sand with the other components, too. Moisture is very important. Spray plants every day and immerse—all over—once a week. Temperatures as high as 90 degrees and as low as 65 degrees are satisfactory; yet utmost care must be taken about moisture when specimens are grown in the higher temperatures. As plants grow taller the pitchers become smaller and assume less interesting shapes. To offset this defect, keep pinching out new growth, and in this way you will produce larger and more highly colored pitchers. Give the plants good light but keep them out of the sun at all times.

Nepenthes may be grown from seed; yet the process involves knowledge of procedure and conditions seldom found in window gardens. Amateurs are advised against attempting it. For first trial it is advisable to purchase established plants with developed pitchers.

ORCHID

family, Orchidaceae

An enormous family of plants with probably the most spectacular flowers to be found anywhere in the world. These beautiful herbs are of two general types, aerial and terrestrial. Most tropical orchids are epiphytes (tree-perching), while temperate and northern-zone species usually are to be found growing on the ground in woodlands or bogs. There are some 7500 species and countless hybrids. One orchid, vanilla, is of vast economic importance; other orchids are commercially valuable for the price their blossoms command in the flower marts.

Northern gardens contain many hardy orchids, such as the ladyslipper genus (*Cypripedium;* there are tender tropical cypripediums, too); and bog gardens are enlivened with the beauty of arethusa, calopogon, calypso, habenaria, orchis, pogonia, etc. Yet it is the showy, flamboyant tropical orchids which are of most interest as house plants.

As a rule indoor gardeners think that orchids require special greenhouse culture in order to grow healthy plants and to enjoy the exquisite flowers. In some instances this is true; yet there are many tropical species and their hybrids which respond readily to growing conditions easily provided for in the average home.

Before going into details, let me give you the experience of two amateur orchid enthusiasts living in a New York apartment house, where conditions are more inimical to orchid culture than might be expected in most private homes.*

* Reprinted from *Horticulture,* by permission the Mass. Horticultural Soc.

"Perhaps it is because we had not lived in the country for many years that the flower growing hunger began to grow on us. It became most acute several years ago and we made up our minds we would grow flowering plants in our apartment. We wanted, however, to do something a little different and started with tuberous-rooted begonias. Then we became orchid conscious. First we brought home a young seedling orchid, the name of which we did not know. The owner of the greenhouse who sold it to us did not know either, other than that it was a cattleya hybrid.

"With only a meager knowledge of its care, we went to work on that orchid. We knew it needed humidity and so we suspended it just above a soup plate half-filled with stones and water, and set it in an east window of our bedroom. We watched the plant very carefully, not only as to shade, but with regard to watering. Very soon, root growths and a new leaf began to appear. Naturally we were delighted with our success. The plant has been repotted twice and is still growing. We are hoping for a blossom on the growth now forming. We have named this first child of our floral family 'Orphan Annie.' It is our hope that when the flower finally makes its appearance, we shall be able to determine what it is.

" 'Orphan Annie's' response to our care gave us the courage to go farther. After studying catalogues and some books on orchid culture, we bought more plants, which have delighted us with their growth and flowers. Today, the collection numbers almost 30 plants, consisting of cattleya species and hybrids, laeliocattleyas, *Odontoglossum grande,* cypripediums, and cymbidiums.

"As this is being written, two cattleyas, *Laeliocattleya schroederae alba,* and two cypripediums are in bloom, all vying with one another. *Cypripedium maudiae,* which joined the collection last winter, is next in line to delight us, while the *Laeliocattleya,* G. S. Ball, a recent acquisition, should put on its show within a week or two. We shall then expect *Cypripedium mossiae* to produce a corsage. Next fall we will be looking forward to the performance of the cypripedium, Brenda and *Cypripedium labiata rosea,* together with some contemplated new members of the groups.

"The present home of our floral family is a window in the bedroom of our apartment. This is on East 89th Street in New York. We had a shelf constructed on top of the radiator enclosure, increasing its depth to about 20 inches. On this shelf are metal pans of different lengths and widths but, in each case, approximately $2\frac{3}{4}$ inches deep. Each pan is provided with a metal grille fitted in the top to support the pots. Linoleum pads under the pans protect the painted surfaces from water.

"In the bottom of each pan there is a sheet of asbestos about one inch thick. This is kept moist at all times to provide humidity. The space between the top of the asbestos and the grille above it is ample to allow free circulation of air around the bottom of the pots.

"We were fortunate in that the window provided two exposures, south and west, and as there are radiators under each section of the window, heat can be controlled satisfactorily. It is thus possible to maintain a warm end and a cool end. Shade is provided and regulated with Venetian blinds

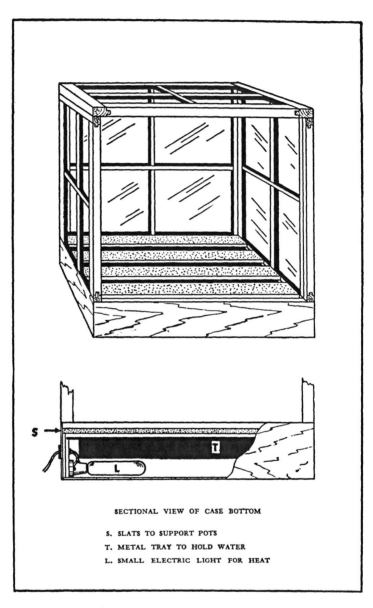

SECTIONAL VIEW OF CASE BOTTOM

S. SLATS TO SUPPORT POTS
T. METAL TRAY TO HOLD WATER
L. SMALL ELECTRIC LIGHT FOR HEAT

FIG. 4   SMALL ORCHID HOUSE

and curtains made of water-repellent silk. Air is controlled by the casement sash.

"Three or four combination thermometers and humidi-guides tell us at all times the temperature and humidity percentage. Thus far we have had no difficulty in maintaining a temperature range between 55 degrees at the cool end, and 60 degrees on the warm end at night, with a maximum day temperature of 70 to 80 degrees.

"We have no set schedule for watering. Watching the plants and the humidity gauge closely tells us when to use the syringe and water. Sunday morning, however, is set aside for examination, watering, washing, and cleaning each plant. We have so far had no trouble with pests of any kind. Only one plant has been lost so far and that, a cypripedium, was the victim of utter carelessness.

"None of these observations will sound very difficult to an orchid expert. But they should imply no difficulty to any flower lover either, if he will go to a little trouble to achieve such beauty for his home . . ."

Certain orchids require more specific control of heat and humidity than may be realized with open-room culture. For the more ambitious window gardener, Fig. 4 shows a small, easily constructed orchid house wherein almost any of the dwarfer orchid plants may be grown.

The top of the device is hinged to allow control of admission and circulation of air. A removable, or hinged, glass door should be provided for the front of the house (not shown in the drawing). Plant containers rest on the floor-slats; beneath is a metal pan and an electric light bulb to provide heat when needed. Water in the pan and pieces of broken flower pots supply essential humidity. The most inexpensive way to construct a small orchid house of this type is to make use of standard glazed window sashes, which may be purchased from a local lumber dealer in almost any shape or size. Completed houses, similar to the one illustrated, are on the market for those who prefer a custom built container.

Unless one has had some experience with these glorious flowers, the list of species and hybrids seems interminable; it is confusing to know where, and with what, to start. The following orchids are suggested to the novitiate for beauty of bloom, ease and economy of purchase, and because their growing proclivities are less likely to discourage the amateur than are some other members of the family: *Cattleya gaskelliana, Cattleya* hybrids (many seedling plants may be acquired at small cost), *Cattleya labiata, Cattleya mossiae, Cattleya percivaliana, Cattleya trianae, Cypripedium harrisianum, Cypripedium insigne, Cypripedium maudiae, Dendrobium superbum, Miltonia vexillaria, Oncidium varicosum.*

CULTURE: Here are given only the major points to be considered in growing tender orchids. These instructions are comprehensive enough for the plants recommended above. If further delving into orchid culture is contemplated, it is advisable to acquire a good book on the subject and—still more important—make friends with a greenhouse operator who is growing orchids as a business. There is more information to be gleaned from such a contact than from all books on the subject put together.

Orchids will not tolerate much sun. See that they get good light yet keep the plants away from direct sun rays. Containers must be absolutely clean and contain more drainage material than is ordinarily required, for constant watering is necessary. The potting mixture for orchids is chopped fern root (osmunda). Each container needs two-thirds osmunda and one-third drainage layer.

An abundance of water is necessary during the growing period, and all plants should be syringed on bright days. Keep the humidity high at all times and see that lots of air is supplied. After active growth has slowed down less water is required, yet plants should continue to receive a light sprinkling often enough to prevent shriveling of the bulbous growths.

Fresh air is not only beneficial but necessary in orchid culture. At the same time, it is important to see that the specimens are kept away from strong air currents—they are fatal.

Ground-growing orchids require less time for resting than the tree-perching species. Some terrestrial genera need no rest period at all. However, most epiphytal orchids do demand the benefit of a quiet period between active growing seasons.

It is a good idea to sponge plants occasionally with a neutral soap and water to destroy any possibility of insect invasion.

As has been mentioned before, these cultural notes are crude and general. It is always advisable to ask for specific information of the seedsman or florist from whom you purchase your plants.

OSMANTHUS

family, Oleaceae

The tea, or sweet olive is not a true olive, although it belongs to the olive family. Members of this group are small
trees or evergreen shrubs widely grown out of doors in
warmer sections of the United States for the pronounced
fragrance of the flowers. One Asiatic species makes a splendid house plant, though rarely used as such.

DESCRIPTION: *Osmanthus fragrans.* The fragrant olive begins to flower when less than 1 foot in height. Leaves are
1¾-4 inches long, usually smooth-edged but occasionally
slightly toothed. Flowers are white, very small, and borne
in the leaf axils usually; they are intensely fragrant and are
produced almost continuously.

CULTURE: The potting mixture best suited to osmanthus
consists of: two parts humus; two parts sand; two parts rich
top soil; one-half part old cow manure. The plant requires
cool growing temperature during the winter months, about
50 degrees. Good drainage is essential and rather sparse
watering. Rest for a month either during the summer or
late in the winter. When repotting is necessary, use a container just one size larger than the one previously used.
Osmanthus is particularly free from insect infestation.

OXALIS

family, Oxalidaceae

The wood sorrels comprise a genus of about 300 species
of dwarfish herbs, several of which are favorite and time-

honored house plants. All have clover-like leaves and
5-petalled flowers in various colors. Oxalis is a cosmopolitan
clan, having representatives from South Africa to South
America, Mexico, and North America. Mostly, the plants
grow from small bulbs or tuberous roots.

Some of the summer-flowering species and varieties make
excellent garden plants, while a number of winter-blooming
oxalis grace thousands of window gardens. It is not the
purpose of this entry to go into details about old favorites
such as Bermuda Buttercup, Grand Duchess, *adenophyla,*
bowieana, rubra, etc., but to suggest a species only recently
offered for sale. It is a lovely pot plant and should be grown
widely.

DESCRIPTION: *Oxalis variabilis.* Grows from a small bulb.
Very large, long-lived flowers of pure pink with primrose
centers are produced in profusion. Blossoms may be enjoyed
from September until the following April. The leaves make
a dense mat of green, just above which the flowers are carried
on short stems.

CULTURE: Plant the bulbs, several to a small pot, in regular
lily potting mixture. Be frugal with watering until growth
has commenced; and, by the way, growth should be started
in a semi-dark location. When indications of budding are
noticed, apply manure water every three or four weeks.
After flowering, the leaves will gradually ripen off, after
which time the bulbs should be rested—in the containers—
for about three months. Oxalis will grow in sun or partial
shade, yet the blossoms last longer and retain the color better
when kept out of direct sun. Prior to budding, sun is beneficial to the plants.

PAROCHETUS

family, Leguminosae

Parochetus is indigenous to Tropical Asia and parts of Africa. It is a handsome herbaceous plant with trailing characteristics and lovely, pea-like flowers. It grows from a thready rhizome and does very well as a house plant.

DESCRIPTION: *Parochetus communis.* The blue oxalis, as the plant is called commonly, grows 2-3 inches high. Leaves resemble those of the shamrock but are marked at the base with a deep brown crescent. Flowers are blue, cobalt blue, with pink wings; they are ½-¾ inch wide, and are produced in leaf axils.

CULTURE: Plant in March or April in a hanging basket or pot. Use regular amaryllis potting mixture. Water regularly and supply manure water while buds are being formed. No resting period required. New plants are acquired easily by root division.

PYRACANTHA

family, Rosaceae

The fire-thorns are a group of thorny, evergreen shrubs native to Asia. They are well-known garden plants, notable for clean bright foliage, and particularly for the masses of red and orange berries which stud the branches. There are hardy and tender species in the group which have been used for landscape purposes. Until recently, the genus has not been regarded as adaptable to the window garden. However, a new dwarf variety of pyracantha is now available which is destined, I believe, to become a most welcome pot subject. It has been experimented with in this category and found to be lacking in none of the characteristics which mark a thoroughly satisfactory and desirable house plant.

DESCRIPTION: *Pyracantha duvalli.* This is the name under which a new fire-thorn variety is offered on the market. At a height of 2 feet or less, the plant produces quantities of brilliant, orange-red berries which remain on the little shrub almost all winter. Small white flowers are borne in branched clusters previous to the appearance of fruit. Dark green, glossy leaves provide a handsome background for the glowing berries. Truly, here is a miniature shrub to be acquired and constantly admired.

CULTURE: Plant in regular iris potting mixture, with the addition of a handful of bone meal to each 6 inch pot. No special care is necessary other than to supervise watering and pruning when needed. A larger container will be required when the plant becomes root-bound.

STRELITZIA

family, Musaceae

A most attractive South African genus of the great banana family. Of the 5 or 6 known species, one in particular is grown for its unusual, exotic flowers which command rather high prices at florists. Established plants are bulky, yet may be grown easily in greenhouses, and without too much trouble in a conservatory or window garden. An unforgettable thrill accompanies the first flowering of *Strelitzia reginae*.

DESCRIPTION: *Strelitzia reginae.* Grows from a woody root-stock. The bird-of-paradise plant is noted for its extraordinary blossoms. They are orange and blue, enclosed in 6-8 inch, boat-shaped, purplish bracts, and carried on stout stalks

STRELITZIA

up to 3 feet in height. Leaves are basal, stalked, about 18 inches long and 6 inches wide. Often just the leaves are made use of in flower arrangements, as they are most decorative and have typically individual characteristics.

CULTURE: Plant the rootstocks in a potting mixture of: two parts fibrous loam; one part peat; one part leaf mold; and sufficient sand to keep the mixture loose and open in texture. Lots of water is required during the summer months, and at no time allow the temperature to cool below 60 degrees. Humidity, too, is welcome. Growing plants, purchased at greenhouses, will be planted in the proper potting soil, probably. However, it is just as well to check on this point. No resting period is required, although less water is needed for a period after the plant has bloomed. Pot-bound roots will hasten flowering, but do not expect blooms on young plants.

WACHENDORFIA

family, Haemodoraceae

A small, South African genus of moisture-loving plants growing from short, thick, tuberous roots. A few species and varieties are in cultivation, mostly with flower spikes not unlike those of delphinium in appearance. Late summer-flowering.

DESCRIPTION: *Wachendorfia thyrsiflora.* A rather coarse, yet attractive plant with 3-foot panicles of bright yellow flowers, and large, plaited leaves. The species remains in flower for a long time. This is the wachendorfia most commonly offered by growers. A smaller species, *Wachendorfia paniculata,* is listed occasionally in catalogues. I do not know where any of the varieties may be obtained in the United States; and it is quite unlikely that they may be imported for some time to come.

CULTURE: Plant the tubers in arum potting mixture, and make sure of ample provision for drainage, as wachendorfia must be kept moist—but not soggy—at all times. Start growth in a darkened location. Grow in the sun until buds have formed, then shade partially. Rest the tubers after the flowering period has been over for several weeks.

Perhaps this is just as good a place as any in the book to mention the omission of any reference to cacti and other succulents. Although these specialists' and hobbyists' plants are of very definite value in the window garden, there are so many excellent books available on the particular subject that I feel what space there is in this book may be utilized better in describing plants about which less literature is extant.

VII

HERBS IN THE HOUSE

SILVER-BELL TREE (*Halesia carolina*). Page 220

CORNELIAN CHERRY (*Cornus mas*). Page 218

Schismatoglottis boebelini. Page 68

Chapter 7

HERBS IN THE HOUSE

Do you grow herbs in your garden? If the answer is "yes" this chapter is of little value to you; for undoubtedly you have discovered already the value and pleasure in cultivating these plants in the house as well as out of doors. On the other hand, there are innumerable window gardeners whose horticultural pursuits are limited, perforce, to indoor growing. Members of this group seldom include herbs in their window gardens.

Perhaps it is because there are other more decorative plants, both in foliage and bloom, to use in window gardens; particularly when space is limited. Yet in many houses and apartments there are window areas available in kitchens, pantries, or spare rooms where small winter herb gardens may be cultivated with esthetic and culinary profit to the grower. Such plantings need not occupy space allocated to the regular window garden.

It is inadvisable to attempt extensive plantings at the outset, either as to quantity or species. Try a few favorites and see how the idea appeals to you. Then what plants you undertake to grow may be determined upon by usable space and personal interest in the various herbs.

Give the indoor herb garden a southern exposure if possible. Plantings that face east or west are satisfactory usually; but, in winter, light from the north is not sufficient for most of the plants.

Helen Noyes Webster says of sweet herbs for the window garden: "The forcing of sweet herbs for house plants or continuing their summer growth into the cold months is not new. Woven into their histories since the days when hospitable Baucis scrubbed her table with fresh mint before bidding the stranger eat at her board, are quaint superstitions and bits of folk lore referring to their attributes as house plants.

"The Colonial housewife stripped fresh sage for cheese and rue leaves for bruises as today we nip off the parsley leaves from our own potted plants in the kitchen window. In Hindu dwellings the pot of basil warded off evil, and in compliment to the departing guest the English cottager still presents this plant from her window's store.

"Sweet marjoram and rosemary were favorites of castle casements, and there is no sweeter plant for the window of a modern home than that rose-of-the-sea, *Rosmarinus officinalis*. Once started, this nearly evergreen perennial shrub should be treasured, reverently pruned, and its pot sunk each spring by a warm sheltered wall or hedge. It must be brought in before September nights become too cold and it always seems to grow better if a bit pot-bound. It is a lime-loving plant and fresh earth worked in with fine plaster rubble invigorates its growth into new green tips all winter.

Only, as the legend runs, 'Never will rosemary grow higher than the Savior's head and only after 33 years will your rose marie increase in breadth.' March suns cover the stems with tiny flowers blue as the Virgin's robe—flowers over which the Mother flung her linen in the flight into Egypt.

"The basils were favorite kitchen herbs of olden days. The little red bush of *Ocimum minimum* is more decorative than its taller broad-leaved cousin, *O. basilicum*. If seeds are sown in August, these quick-growing herbs will live on our plant shelf their allotted span of annual life—perhaps until January. The pungent oil-filled leaves give zest to our fish sauces, also the tomato cookery 'and procure unto their host a cheerful and a merry heart!'

"Other annual sweet herbs which survive with more or less frailty our New England indoor winters are coriander, dill, and the small fragrant fennel. Like basil they are at home in rich friable soil and if we do not wish to transplant the half-grown plants in September it is easy to circumvent that difficulty by making August sowing of seeds in permanent receptacles. These may be tin cans with holes punched in the bottom, or if you are ambitious, glazed pottery in unique shape and color. The roots dry out too quickly in the ordinary flower pot and an outer container is likely to hold standing water, a disastrous condition for these little plants.

"French sorrel, parsley, and the perennial fennel, *Foeniculum vulgare,* are treated alike. It is useless to transplant old plants. They have tough, unyielding tap roots, but by selecting very young plants and putting them in deep pots, which are left out of doors until cold weather, we obtain satisfactory house plants. The crowns thicken and grow the new green leaves, which increase in a most entertaining fashion as we cull the outer varieties for our dishes and salads. But if the soil dries out in porous pots and frequent sprayings be forgotten, insect pests will mitigate our joy in their possession.

"Tarragon, chives, mints, and sweet balm, *Melissa officinalis,* are grand kitchen-window house plants, if the atmosphere is entirely free from gas, which is eventual death to all herbs; although lavender, balm, and several thymes are surprisingly tolerant. *Mentha requieni* gives up its life on the instant; likewise the mountain thyme. Warm, sunny windows and fresh air are their joy.

"The most exquisite house plant that ever was mine was a low bulb pot of lamb mint, *Mentha viridis.* It came from a network of underground stems which I had dug up in September. Until early December this pot of mint had remained forgotten in a bed of leaves under the rhododendrons. Then I found it snowed under and the earth frozen. Undaunted, ever confident in the surprises with which sweet herbs repay their hosts, I carried the pot of mint into the laundry, gave it a long gentle ducking in a tub of cold water and later the warmth of a cool sunny window.

"The awakening was heralded one morning in January when at its daily watering that all-pervading minty fragrance assailed my nostrils. The buried root stalks had budded into stiff little leaves which soon gathered greenness and increased in numbers. It was a fascinating centerpiece of which Gerard, the old herbalist of the 16th century who found some good in every plant of God's creation, might have said again, 'The smell rejoiceth the heart of man for which cause they used to strew it in chambers of recreation, pleasure and repose, where feasts and banquets are made.'

"Blue-blossoming Jill-over-the-ground, *Nepeta hederacea,* is as pretty a trailer for a hanging basket as any more conventional exotic. Young plants of lavender, sage and santolina, lavender cotton, are sweet herbs, precious as house plants, and they link us in memory with gardens of long ago. They are charming in glazed pottery of tints reflecting their various hues of green and gray. But of all our window herbs, who will not love best all the fragrant thymes? The 'carpenters,' woolly, mountain, and lemon thyme, must have shallow dishes in which to creep and if these have no outlet, drainage may be secured by an inch of lime rubble under the potting soil.

"For window 'stands' (those galvanized boxes set in wickerwork) the best varieties for indoor winter cultivation are *Thymus vulgaris,* the common garden thyme, *Thymus fragrantissimus,* or that now popular little bush, *Thymus erectus.* They should be set fairly close with a plant or two of citron or nutmeg geranium and perhaps old 'lurk-in-the-ditch' which is the English name for pennyroyal.

"Fresh air above all else these herb plants must have, for their ancestors revelled in the sun and the breezes. Often there comes a breathless sunny day in February. Joy be to the herbs! Open wide the windows and let them bathe in ozone. The thymes are blossoming and their purple pitchers lure an early honey bee who drifts lazily into the room on its first flight of the year from the somnolent hive. As it hovers over the fragrance of the thyme flowers, we see again

the 'emblem which in days of old, fine ladies embroidered on
their cavaliers' scarves'—a honey bee hovering over a sprig
of thyme, the little plant symbolic of activity, bravery, and
courage.

"There is a device, the 'sunlight shelf,' which is attached
to brackets screwed on the window casing about halfway up.
The shelf is broad and stands about six inches from the window's glass. It makes an ideal garden for sweet herbs. This
shelf has inch-high sides and a galvanized pan fits exactly
inside. It may be filled with peat in which small pots are set
saucerless, or it may have merely a layer of pebbles to insure drainage and dampness.

"The low-growing herbs, thymes, camomile, and dwarf
lavenders, that love the hot sun, are set along the edge nearest
the window. The fragrant little mint likes shade and the
edges of the shelf under pots of rue and sweet marjoram.
Along the center are the plants of dill, fennel, coriander,
anise, and basil. On the outer edge of the shelf, swinging
their fragrance into the room, are the trailing stems of mints,
and there is just enough sunlight sifting through the other
plants to keep their leaves from yellowing. Their stems
against the window pane make an entrancing lower curtain.
Here also we put the chives, tarragon, and lemon balm.
Loveliest of all, on the very ends and against the window
casings, place your rosemarys, with their lax stems held up
by miniature trellises.

"Dispense with the conventional upper window shade
and make two short draw curtains of waterproof material,
quaintly patterned. If these are made to slip easily on rings

they may be drawn between the plant shelf and the window pane when the plants are sprayed or on cold nights.

"I am frequently asked, 'Which herbs do you use most, or what do you use them for anyway?' At one time or another I use them all—for salads, seasonings, and winter nosegays. Esthetically they please our senses and challenge our superstitions." *

In the discussion above, Mrs. Webster has accomplished an admirable generalization of window garden herbs. However, for the benefit of those who have had no experience in growing or using these plants, more detailed information on the subject will be welcome, probably.

As a parallel case to the entry on orchids, I would like to call attention to the fact that when interest in indoor herb culture has extended beyond the embryo stage, there is an extensive range of literature extant—articles, pamphlets, and books patterned to meet the most casual or exacting inquiries. This chapter does not purport to be a monograph on the subject of herbs; it is written with the hope of enthusing indoor gardeners to include some, or many, herbs in house plantings. Seekers for advanced information are referred to the bibliography of horticultural books on page 227.

When considering a choice of herbs to grow indoors, keep in mind that some are annuals, some biennials, and others are perennial in nature. While all may be grown from seed, the initial indoor herb garden is best started with plants which have been purchased or dug from generous neighbors' herb gardens.

* Reprinted from *Horticulture,* by permission the Mass. Horticultural Soc.

Potting soil should be friable in texture and a little on the alkaline side. If lush growth is the primary requisite, have the soil rich in plant food. If the herbs are to be used for flavoring or aroma, a rather poor soil is recommended. In any event supply good drainage. Also, keep plants pinched back to induce bushiness. Until the herbs are established and obviously thriving, keep the potting soil damp; and a daily sprinkling of top growth will help, too.

Herewith follows a description of herbs best suited for growing indoors, together with a few notes on how to use them for other than decorative purposes.

WINDOW GARDEN HERBS

for decoration, aroma, and kitchen-craft

A Few Window Garden Herbs That Are Dependable

ANISE

Pimpinella anisum

A half-hardy annual with yellow or white flowers and delicate, fern-like leaves. The plant grows 12-15 inches in height.

Originally a native of Egypt, the herb is grown everywhere now. Its use for flavoring dates to a period B.C. when Romans made use of the seeds to spice cakes. At present, anise is employed to flavor a certain type of bread, and is the basis of a popular cordial.

Pot the plants late in August and allow them to remain

out of doors in the containers until frost threatens before taking them inside. When they are placed in the window garden, prune back severely.

SWEET BASIL

Ocimum basilicum, or the dark variety, *Ocimum basilicum,* var. *purpureum*

A tender annual with small white or lavender flowers, 1-2 feet in height when fully grown. The clove-like flavor of basil is enjoyed by epicures with rugged tastes, yet it is too peppery and strong for the average palate.

Many superstitions and odd beliefs surround this herb. In the Orient basil still is held sacred. It is a holy herb of the Hindoos, for instance, and is grown throughout India to ward off evil. On the other hand, in many Occidental countries basil was regarded as possessing sinister qualities. Aside from any of these doubtful attributes, the herb makes a splendid plant for the indoor herb garden.

Handle in the same way as anise.

BORAGE

Borago officinalis

A rough-stemmed annual with handsome black-eyed, blue flowers. This is an ancient herb, for in *The Treasurie of Hidden Secrets and Commodious Conceits,* England, 1586, appears the following notation: "The vertue of the conserve of borage is especially good against melancholie: it maketh one merrie."

Soup flavoring was the principal use for young borage leaves; the flowers often were candied, and today the scintillating blue blossoms are lovely in a potpourri.

Pot in late August.

CHERVIL

Anthriscus cerefolium

An annual, 2-foot herb of old lineage and many uses. It has decorative, fern-like leaves and grows from a tuberous root not unlike a carrot in appearance. The flowers are white.

The Romans used chervil and it is mentioned in all the old herbals. Chervil was used as a pot herb, in salads, sauces, and for garnishing. Often the roots were cooked in various ways and eaten with relish. When used for flavoring, the younger the leaves are, the better.

Handle like anise.

CORIANDER

Coriandrum sativum

An annual herb bearing white flowers and growing to 30 inches, although seldom in the house. At present the herb is used for flavoring liquors and liqueurs. Centuries ago, particularly in Egypt and Palestine, dried coriander seeds were crushed and beaten into the bread-mix. The Bible refers to this herb in Exodus xvi, 31: "And the House of Israel called the name thereof Manna: and it was like Coriander seed, white; and the taste of it was like wafers made with honey."

Pot in August and handle like anise.

DILL

Anethum graveolens

A 3-foot annual or biennial with handsome leaves and yellow flowers. An herb with a long heritage of fame. Now used mostly in conjunction with pickling processes.

In more credulous times, dill was one of the herbs regarded as essential by magicians in the fomenting of charms; and as a protection against unfriendly witchcraft.

Handle like anise.

CARAWAY

Carum carui

A hardy biennial. The herb grows 1-2 feet in height and has rather attractive white flowers. The flavor of caraway seeds is too familiar to require any further mention. Either you like it or abhor it!

Treat in the same way as the annual herbs above described.

SWEET FENNEL

Foeniculum officinalis

A biennial herb of large stature, 18 inches to 4 feet, with numerous yellow flowers and feathery leaves. Used medicinally and for flavoring; also as a vegetable.

Handle as above.

Parsley

Petroselinum hortense

A familiar small biennial with dark green, curly leaves. Everyone has admired the touch of decoration parsley adds to a dish of chops or boiled potatoes; yet how many know that the classic Greeks regarded this plant so highly it was used to fabricate a wreath-crown awarded the victor at the Isthmian games.

Pot about the first of September for use inside during the winter.

Lemon Balm

Melissa officinalis

A hardy perennial, 16-24 inches in height. The flowers are white and appear almost continuously. The entire plant has a strong lemon taste and smell.

Balm was a favorite strewing herb in olden days, for foot-crushed leaves release a delightful effluvium. Balm tea is still brewed as a summer drink; it is most refreshing and has an elusive but noticeable lemon flavor. It may be served hot or iced.

Pot in late August and cut back severely.

Chives

Allium schoenoprasum

This is one of the onion tribe growing from a cluster of small white bulbs. Leaves are round and grass-like; the flower heads are purple. The use of chives for delicate onion flavoring in cooking and salads is well known.

Clumps of chives may be dug and potted at any time. Leave them out of doors in the containers for several weeks before removal to the house.

GERANIUM

Pelargonium varieties

Sweet-scented geraniums find a proper and welcome place in the indoor herb garden. Many different kinds are available; which, in addition to having lovely flowers and interesting leaves, bring to the owner gracious scents of spice, rose, lemon, orange, pineapple, almond, and innumerable other less definable but equally aromatic odors.

Regular geranium culture.

HOREHOUND

Marrubium vulgare

A hardy perennial, 1-3 feet in height. The plant is quite shrubby and bears whorls of white flowers. Formerly horehound was used to make teas and syrups; now it is used principally as the flavoring element in horehound candy.

Pot in September and cut back severely.

LAVENDER

Lavandula officinalis

Lavender is a "must" in any herb garden, whether inside

or out. While there are numerous species and varieties of lavender, the true sweet lavender is the best for a window garden.

The plant is a perennial, from 1-3 feet in height, with blue or purple flowers and grayish leaves that are scented deliciously. Bags of dried lavender leaves are used widely in drawers and cupboards to scent linens.

Dig and pot in September, following the usual admonition to prune back.

MINT

Mentha species

Of the numerous mints, three are recommended for the indoor garden. All are desirable and will pleasantly aromatize any locale in which they are grown.

Mentha gentilis. The golden apple mint is a perennial creeping plant which may be utilized as a trailer.

Mentha piperita, var. *officinalis.* Peppermint. A hardy perennial, 1-3 feet in height, with spicate purple flowers.

Mentha spicata. Spearmint. A hardy perennial, 1-2 feet high, with spikes of purple flowers. The entire plant is very strongly scented.

Dig and pot in the late fall. The mints require treatment different from that prescribed for herbs previously mentioned. After potting, allow plants to remain out of doors *until the roots have frozen solid.* Then take into the house and new growth will appear soon. Also, mints prefer a heavy soil and copious watering; yet they will not tolerate sour soil, so watch out for drainage and standing water in saucers.

ROSEMARY

Rosemarinus officinalis

A scented perennial herb, 2-4 feet in height. The numerous narrow leaves are gray-green in color; flowers are small but of an exquisite shade of blue. Together with lavender, rosemary is the finest of fragrant herbs.

At one time rosemary was regarded highly for its efficacy in warding off infection; and it was dried and burned as incense; which use might well be continued today, for the scent is most agreeable and lasting.

Dig, pot, and prune in September.

SAGE

Salvia officinalis

Garden sage is a gray-leaved perennial herb with white or purplish flowers. It grows to a height of 12-16 inches.

For more years than there are bees in a hive sage has been noted for its remarkable health-giving and restoring properties. Today it is a standard spice, used universally in cheese and poultry dressings.

Dig and pot in late August. Pruning is unnecessary, although no harm comes from doing so.

THYME

Thymus species

The thymes are shrubby or creeping aromatic perennials, almost legion in the number of species and varieties recognized. Out of the convention of thymes, two come forward as excellent subjects for the indoor herb garden; although you may grow any or all if you wish.

Legend decrees that thyme was the fairies' favorite herb; and keepers of apiaries in olden times expressed the opinion that—"the owners of hives have a perfite foresight and knowledge of what the increase or yielde of Honey will bee everie yeare by the plentifull or small number of flowers growing and appearing in the Thyme about the summer solstice."

Thymus serpyllum, var. *citriodorus.* The lemon thyme makes mats of attractive green leaves from which arise stalks of red-bracted, pink flowers. A persistent lemon scent is noticeable at all times. The plant is a low-growing perennial.

Thymus vulgaris. The shrubby garden thyme flowers profusely and is strongly scented. Like the variety above it is a perennial, but is larger and stronger in all its parts. Out of doors it is almost evergreen. This is the species most often used for flavoring. For a clean delightful clothes or fur perfume, try a mixture of dried rosemary and thyme leaves with freshly ground cloves. You will enjoy the scent but the moths will not.

Dig and pot in late August.

The herbs recommended in this chapter are but a small selection of plants which may be grown in the window garden. Those listed have been chosen because they are almost sure to be satisfactory indoors. There are other herbs, of course, many suitable for indoor culture.

If you continue to grow an indoor herb garden year after year, undoubtedly you will try all the herbs eventually.

VIII

MAGIC WANDS

Chapter 8

MAGIC WANDS

A<small>NY GROWING</small> thing is welcome in late winter and early spring. Flowers and foliage of house plants seem doubly valuable at this time. Yet no matter how interesting or beautiful the pot specimen may be, there is an indeterminate feeling of something lacking. Perhaps it is latent nostalgia for the more homely and commonplace plants which blossom later in the garden or orchard or border.

Winter plant beauty need not be confined to pots. A preview of approaching spring is often a joy, for January and February represent neap tide in the northern gardener's year. While stirrings of new plant life are taking place underground, all that is visible is bleak and winter-bound, locked in a seemingly interminable ice-grip. Annuals are hiding within brown seed cases; perennials exhibit nothing but skeleton stalks of the previous year. Cheerful green of foliage, beauty and fragrance of flowers; at no time are they more welcome than at the tag end of winter.

We may look to flowering shrubs and trees for an answer to the problem. Already sap is beginning to creep within them; little effort is required to hasten the flow of life fluid and cause bare branches to become fringed with leaf-green and bright blossoms.

Cut branches will respond, in a fashion, to almost any forcing attention. Yet some knowledge and care about the ins and outs of forcing procedure will result in more pleasing and satisfactory results.

Plan to cut the wands on a day when the temperature has crawled above freezing. If it is raining, so much the better, for moisture helps buds to swell and sap to flow. Long branches are preferable to short sprays; flowers are more perfectly formed and last longer. Linear area is a measure of sap content; and sap—lots of it—is essential to complete forcing. When the required number of cut branches has been collected, place them in a filled bath tub and allow them to remain there overnight. Have the water in the tub just above room temperature. After soaking, re-move 3 or 4 inches of bark from the cut ends, and the branches are ready for jars and vases. At this point charcoal becomes a most useful adjunct. If several pieces are dropped into the container when it is filled, only water dissipated by evaporation need be replaced; otherwise stagnancy will ne-cessitate periodical cleaning and a new supply of water. A weekly spray of tepid water will be of material assistance in the swelling and opening of dormant buds.

Temperature, too, is an important factor in successful forc-ing. The usual procedure is to bring cut branches into the house, place them in containers, and distribute the containers wherever wanted. Most rooms, at this season of the year, are kept at 70-75 degrees to combat the intense cold outside. Such a temperature unduly hastens opening of buds and results in dwarfed or imperfectly formed flowers of disappointingly short life. Many branch-cuttings, forced under these conditions, progress splendidly until flower buds are just at the point of opening. Then nothing further happens. Soon the bud clusters droop and dry off, leaving nothing but bare twigs or leaves to satisfy weeks of expectancy.

No, a cool place is necessary, but not too cool. A spot where the temperature is between 60-65 degrees. And where is the house wherein there does not exist such a location? A pantry, a sunporch, a room with a temperamental radiator; somewhere in *your* house there is just the right place, where the temperature and three to five hours of sun daily will provide the proper combination of forcing conditions.

Some of the branches which you will use produce flowers before the leaves appear; others send forth leaves prior to flowers. In either case allow branches to remain in the cool location until *flower* buds are just ready to open. Then the wands may be distributed throughout the house as you choose.

Only shrubs and trees on which flower buds have formed before cuttings are taken may be expected to blossom in the house.

Forcing at cool temperatures requires more time between cutting and flowering; yet the additional wait is justified in the light of increased perfection and longevity. While it is inadvisable to attempt any forcing before January, the earlier in the season branches are cut, the more imperative it is to force in cool locations. Later, when sap is normally active and buds are swelling out of doors, the matter of forcing-temperature becomes increasingly unimportant.

Listed herewith are a number of flowering shrubs and
trees which have proved amenable to branch-forcing in late
winter. There are others, of course; yet those listed require
the least effort and skill to produce pleasing results.

TREES AND SHRUBS FOR BRANCH-FORCING INDOORS

Acer rubrum

RED MAPLE

Normal flowering period, March-April. Brilliant red flowers stud the branches before the leaves appear. A familiar
and beloved tree of the lowlands and swamps.

Aesculus hippocastanum

COMMON HORSECHESTNUT

No flowers appear on forced branches, but the delicate new
leaves, as they unfurl, are most interesting and welcome as
spots of living green.

Alnus

THE ALDERS

Flowers in this genus appear before the leaves and consist
of catkins; male and female growing on the same tree or
shrub. Later in the spring, female catkins become small,
woody cones.

Amygdalus

THE PEACHES

Small, charming pink flowers produced in profusion. Be sure to cut branches bearing flower buds. Peaches bear flowers on previous year's wood; and buds appear in pairs usually, with a smaller leaf bud between.

Berberis

THE BARBERRIES

All the barberries are spring-blooming. Yellow flowers appear in loose or close clusters. Wood of branches, too, is yellow in color. The leaves are small and bright green.

Betula

THE BIRCHES

Flowers appear early in the spring as catkins. Female flowers are cone-like, bracted clusters. Branches force early and easily.

Caragana arborescens

SIBERIAN PEA TREE

The yellow, pea-like flowers are about ¾ inch long; several borne closely together. Forced branches are very showy.

Cercis canadensis

AMERICAN REDBUD

The redbud is a member of the pea family. Flowers are rosy-pink, carried in clusters of 4-8 blossoms, and there are numerous clusters. Varieties include a white and a double-flowered pink form.

Chionanthus virginica

FRINGE TREE

Flowers are very large and showy, white, and borne in hanging clusters about 7 inches in length. Individual petals are 1-2 inches long.

Cornus

THE DOGWOODS

Many of the cornels or dogwoods provide good branch-cuttings for forcing in water. Note particularly *Cornus florida,* its pink variety, and the next entry.

Cornus mas

CORNELIAN CHERRY

In March or April this cornus produces numerous small yellow flowers on naked twigs. Excellent for forcing, and a fine shrub to grow in the border or woody screen.

Corylopsis

Related to the witch-hazels. Nodding clusters of yellow flowers are produced before leaves appear. Either *Corylopsis spicata* or *Corylopsis pauciflora* may be used.

Chaenomeles japonica (Cydonia japonica)

JAPANESE FLOWERING QUINCE

The red flowers of this small shrub are well known in many gardens. In addition to the above species, there are horticultural varieties with pink, white, and lemon-tinted blossoms.

Deutzia gracilis

DEUTZIA

Smallest and most desirable of the deutzias for forcing. It has numerous clusters of pure white flowers, each blossom about ¾ inch wide. The variety, *Deutzia rosea,* has bell-shaped flowers of pink.

Forsythia

GOLDEN BELL

No comment necessary on these widely used shrubs. All species and varieties force readily.

Halesia carolina

SILVER-BELL TREE

Also called the snowdrop tree. Clusters of bell-shaped, white flowers. Fine, and should be used more often for indoor bloom.

Hamamelis japonica

JAPANESE WITCH-HAZEL

Yellow flowers, about ¾ inch long, appear from January to March. Do not confuse this plant with *Hamamelis virginiana,* the common witch-hazel, as the latter flowers in the autumn.

Hamamelis mollis

CHINESE WITCH-HAZEL

Quite similar to *Hamamelis japonica,* but the flowers are golden-yellow, touched with red at the base. Blooms normally February-March.

Kerria japonica

KERRIA

This shrub, and the variety, *Kerria japonica pleniflora,* have large yellow to orange flowers, borne at the ends of short lateral branches. The bark is bright green.

Lonicera fragrantissimus

BUSH HONEYSUCKLE

There are numerous bush honeysuckles. Of them all, the creamy-white, intensely fragrant flowers of this Chinese immigrant are the best for forcing.

Malus

THE APPLES

Branches of all the apples make satisfactory indoor subjects. Be sure to cut twigs and branches with flower buds on them.

Philadelphus

THE MOCKORANGES

All the species and varieties usually grown in the shrub border may be used.

Platanus occidentalis

SYCAMORE TREE

Also called the plane or button ball tree. Flowers are small and ball-like, borne in clusters; male and female flowers on the same tree. One writer describes them as resembling fuzzy little lemons.

Prunus americana

WILD PLUM

The wild or yellow plum has numerous small clusters of white flowers, usually about 1 inch in width.

Prunus avium

COMMON SWEET CHERRY

Branches are covered with clusters of white flowers.

Prunus domestica

COMMON PLUM

Numerous flowers of greenish-white appear before the leaves have opened fully.

Prunus glandulosa

FLOWERING ALMOND

Attractive flowers of pink or white, produced in quantity and resembling small rosettes.

Prunus subhirtella

JAPANESE ROSEBUD CHERRY

Light pink flowers about 1 inch wide, with notched petals and almost countless in numbers. There are many varieties of Japanese flowering cherries, most of which are excellent for forcing.

Pyrus

THE PEARS

The same information noted under malus applies here.

Ribes

THE CURRANTS

Depending upon the species or variety used, flowers may be greenish-white, greenish-brown, greenish-purple, green, yellow, or red. The flowering currant, *Ribes sanguineum,* has particularly showy clusters of large flowers.

Salix discolor

COMMON PUSSY WILLOW

No comment needed here, except to mention that the goat willow, *Salix caprea,* and its horticultural varieties provide larger, handsomer "pussies."

Spiraea thunbergi

SPIREA

Of the numerous spiraeas, this is the one that will prove most satisfactory for early forcing. *Spiraea prunifolia,* the true bridal wreath, is almost as amenable and well worth using, too.

Staphylea trifolia

AMERICAN BLADDER-NUT

An interesting shrub from which to cut branches for forcing. The flowers are white or greenish-white; rather inconspicuous, foliage decorative.

If you are fortunate enough to grow, or have access to, a plant of *Staphylea colchica,* you may have flowers of exquisite waxy-white, heavily scented. This is the handsomest of the bladder-nuts, and the first to bloom. Not widely grown.

Perhaps you wonder why such a common shrub as lilac has not been included in this listing. Small branches of lilac do not force well. Bud-clusters form easily enough, yet usually wither before opening. On the other hand, branches 6 feet or more in length, placed in buckets of water, will flower nicely. Yet who wants to injure a fine lilac bush by removing cuttings of this size?

OTHER BOOKS OF INTEREST TO INDOOR GARDENERS

Arrangement, Creative Flower, Dorothy Biddle and E. D. Blom

Arrangement, Flower, F. F. Rockwell and Esther G. Grayson

Arrangement, Japanese Flower, Margaret Preininger

Begonias and How to Grow Them, Bessie R. Buxton

Begonias, Tuberous-rooted, George Otten

Bulbs and House Plants, C. H. Matschat

Bulbs for Your Garden, Allen H. Wood, Jr.

Cactus Book, The, A. D. Houghton

Cacti, Our Native, Ethel Bailey Higgins

Cactus, Culture, Ellen D. Schulz

Chemical Gardening for the Amateur, C. H. Connors and V. A. Tiedjens

Chemical Gardening, Growing Plants in Nutrient Solutions, W. I. Turner and V. M. Henry

Chemical Gardening, Soilless Growth of Plants, C. Ellis and M. W. Swaney

Chemical Gardening, Complete Guide to Soilless Gardening, Dr. Wm. F. Gericke

Dish Gardening, Patten Beard
Gardeners' Omnibus, The, E. I. Farrington
Greenhouse, Gardening in the, Anne Dorrance
Herbs and Herb Gardening, Eleanour Sinclair Rohde
Herbs for Flavor and Fragrance, Gardening With, Helen Morgenthau Fox
Herbs: How to Grow Them and Use Them, Helen Noyes Webster
Home Flower Growing, Emil C. Volz
House Plants, Grow Them Indoors, Allen H. Wood, Jr.
House Plants, Gardening Indoors, F. F. Rockwell and Esther G. Grayson
Orchid Culture, American, E. A. White
Plant Culture, G. W. Oliver and A. C. Hottes
Roof Gardening, Ida Mellen
South African Plants for American Gardens, Sarah V. Coombs
Succulents for the Amateur, Brown, White, Sloane, and Reynolds
Terrariums, Gardens in Glass, Mildred N. Andrews

INDEX TO BOTANICAL NAMES

229

INDEX TO COMMON NAMES

CPSIA information can be obtained at www.ICGtesting.com
Printed in the USA
LVOW081435271212

313474LV00004B/113/P